The Colour of God

A Story of Family and Faith

Ayesha Siddiqua Chaudhry

ONEWORLD

A Oneworld Book

First published by Oneworld Publications in 2021
This paperback edition published 2022

ISBN 978-0-86154-220-8
eISBN 978-1-78607-976-3

Typeset by Hewer Text UK Ltd, Edinburgh
Printed and bound in Great Britain by Clays Ltd, Elcograf S.p.A.

Oneworld Publications
10 Bloomsbury Street
London WC1B 3SR
England

Stay up to date with the latest books,
special offers, and exclusive content from
Oneworld with our newsletter

Sign up on our website
oneworld-publications.com

Praise for *The Colour of God*

'*The Colour of God* is an engrossing read, not because it tells the story of one woman's journey from "subjugation" within a puritanical sect of Islam to finding "liberation" by taking off her veil, but because it refuses and interrogates these facile labels. Chaudhry is brilliant at dissecting how fundamentalism took root in her family, and she's equally good at holding up a mirror to the culture that tends to dehumanise those who don't conform to its norms.'

Monica Ali, author of *Brick Lane*

'*The Colour of God* offers us a sustained exploration of home and belief and the tendrils between the two . . . a beautiful and necessary book that remarkably, wonderfully, makes our world larger and smaller at once.'

Ross Gay, bestselling author of *The Book of Delights*

'The kind of authentic voice that is rarely heard nowadays. Her experiences of family and the patriarchal interpretations of Islam, pushed upon women of South Asian heritage, resonated with me on so many levels.'

Saima Mir, author of *The Khan*

'An exquisite, engrossing, and very moving book.'

New York Journal of Books

'This book fell into my heart, bringing real life, real love, pain and grief... Chaudhry writes beautifully.'

Sabrina Mahfouz

For

Light dancing on titlywings.
My Medina.
Chiryasong of my dil.

صبغة الله ومن أحسن من الله صبغة ﴿۞﴾

The colour of God. And what is better than the colour of God?

—The Qur'an

Contents

What is your name, li'l munna?
                    My name is Sibghatullah.
What does your name mean?
                    The colour of God.
And what is the colour of God?
                    Ummm . . . green, I think . . . or maybe light brown.

PART I

PART I

Anguish

It is not my place to tell his story. Only my own. And my story is formed by him. So, should I start with the day he was born, on a cold, wintry December night, snowflakes drifting lazily in the yellow glow of street lamps? Or with the day he died, on a warm, rainy summer night in June, four and a half years later?

There's no right place to begin, so let's start with his death. His death made me go back and rethink everything. Made me see that the most fundamental facts of life are unstable, shaky. Like time. Time does not just march forward. Sometimes it skips ahead, rushing through long stretches of life, and other times it resists forward motion, moving unbearably slowly, dragging itself out, refusing to move along. Like a puppy resisting the leash, digging his feet into the pavement, preferring to rip his pads than give in to the demands of his walker. And sometimes it loops right back, keeping you stuck in a nightmare from which you cannot wake. Like water endlessly circling the drain, never emptying out. His death floods my mind, it seeps into every corner of my brain, it drenches every memory.

It's June 28, 2005 and I am twenty-four years old. I have been married for about six months. I fought tooth and nail, prayed my heart out to marry this boy, not yet a man. He is two months younger than me. His parents opposed our marriage. They didn't come to the wedding, even though he got on his knees and begged them.

If you marry her, you're not welcome back here, they said, and then followed through. Well, for a few years anyways.

My family was full of trepidation about our wedding, about my marrying a person whose parents disowned him. They wondered aloud if I could trust him. *Does he know what he's doing? Will he change his mind tomorrow?*

Yes, he does and *No, he won't,* I told them, with more confidence than I felt.

We got married in Las Vegas, though that's less scandalous than it sounds. My sister was living there at the time and offered to host the wedding. My parents, my siblings with their growing families and a few friends gathered, taking up too little space in a vast green prayer hall at a mosque just off the Strip. The day was December 18, 2004, Sibghatullah's fourth birthday. Whose bright idea was it for us to get married on his birthday? One of us must have thought up this plan but all of us thrilled at the harmony and beauty of it. Love upon love. Baraka multiplied. His mother, my older sister, single-handedly organised the wedding – made the arrangements at the mosque, booked the reception at a restaurant, made the salon appointments, waxed my legs, arms and face the night before, hosted my entire family of six siblings, spouses, children and parents in her two-bedroom apartment.

Sibghatullah had been involved in all the planning. He had opinions about the hairstyle his mother chose for me, the cake she picked out, the clothes I would wear. He thought that the wedding was his, that he was the one marrying me, and was scandalised to learn that his Ayesha Khala wasn't coming to marry him at all, but some random guy named Rumee. He expressed his disappointment by icing him out. He never really warmed up to Rumee. I'm sure he would have eventually. But there wasn't enough time.

Back to that June evening. I've been married for six months and ten days now and I don't know what I'm doing. I do not understand marriage. I've never been in a romantic relationship before. Neither has Rumee. It took us three weeks to figure out how to have sex. If sex is instinctual, our instincts were buried so deep we didn't know where to look. Rumee's friend advised him, *Just get in there and explode.*

Well, it took a while for him to *get in there.* For weeks, as we tried to figure out what comes naturally to animals, Rumee would ask, *Am I in?* And I'd say, . . . *I think so?*

When he was finally in, we both knew. He didn't ask and I didn't respond with a question. It felt good.

Rumee's parents were not speaking to him. Some of my family members were not speaking to each other. There were several fights before and after the wedding. Sometimes, families use reunions to air their grievances. Some of the fights were over money, as though money could heal years of trauma. When the visit was over, my father departed in a huff, without saying goodbye or hugging Sibghatullah. Even at his young age, he noticed and was hurt.

Why is Nana angry? he asked.

This haughty and momentary lapse on my father's part will haunt us for the rest of our days. Some of our mistakes are carried by those we love.

Six months after the wedding, my older sister is in transit, moving from Las Vegas to a small town in New England. I have just moved myself from New York to Rumee's apartment in Baltimore so that we can play house, but I'm not expecting the relationship to work out. He's working at some nine-to-five job instead of finishing his PhD. I'm at home, all day, preparing for my comprehensive exams. I'm doing a PhD in Islamic Studies at New York University, and on that campus and in that city I had a social network. I have no friends here. There is nowhere to walk. I am eating too much ice-cream.

On June 28th, Rumee convinces me to work out with him at the gym in our apartment complex. I reluctantly agree after much whining about how much I hate sweating. To my twenty-four-year-old mind, sweating is gross and sweating in hijab is more gross. I find fitness clothes obscene, at odds with my notions of modesty. I wear too many clothes when I work out; long yoga pants for jogging, the bottom half of the legs flared so they don't excessively hug my curves. On top I wear a long-sleeved shirt, but this is too revealing and the shape of my butt shows through the yoga pants. To fix both these problems, I wear an extra-large men's cotton T-shirt over my outfit. This hides all my curves, my butt, waist and bust. Now for the head. I tie a small, non-slip cotton kerchief on my head. This will ensure that the hijab I wrap over the kerchief doesn't move from physical exertion. I look in the mirror. *Do I look modest enough?* Rumee thinks so. My mother's voice in my head disagrees. I ignore her and head to the gym.

I climb the elliptical machine and, momentarily, I feel much, much better – the endorphin release eases my gnawing anxiety and distracts me from the judgemental voices in my head. As we are about to head back to the apartment, it starts pouring rain. Hard, East Coast summer rain. Warm and strong. We look at each other and realise there is no way around it, we are going to get drenched. At first, we run with our shoulders hunched, as if to shield us, but pretty soon our apprehension melts into childish glee as we run through the heavy downpour, bodies open, laughing, our clothes wet and heavy, our shoes squelching.

We get home, buzzing with energy as we shower and change into dry, comfortable clothes. I make myself a hot chocolate. Rumee sits to write something at the desk in the den. I curl up on the floor behind him, my legs folded under me as I lean forward to read another book for my exams. I remember the book, *Qur'an, Liberation and Pluralism* by Farid Esack.

At around 10:30P.M. my phone rings. It is a flip phone, my first cell. There is a red light on top that flashes when it rings. I pick up and hear a sound that is impossible to describe but that imprints itself forever in my brain. It is a wail, or a lament, the sound of an animal wounded deeply and irreparably.

Hello? Who is this? I ask tentatively. I look at the number; I don't recognise it. The phone disconnects.

I call the number back and a man answers. He says he is with my older sister. I know immediately that he is a stranger because he mispronounces her name. He gives her the phone. She is wailing, screaming, hysterical.

No, no, no! He's gone! He's gone! Sibghatullah is gone! I want him back, I want my baby back!

What do you mean he's gone? Who took him? Of course you can have him back! I assure her as I frantically try to figure out what is going on.

She hangs up and I feel a wild panic rise within me.

What is going on? I ask Rumee. Who took Sibghatullah? Why did they take him? Was he kidnapped? Was it the government? No thought is outlandish in light of the most outlandish thought of all – that Sibghatullah could be gone. Gone where?

The phone rings again. This call is from Canada, my parents' house. My younger sister is on the phone.

Are you sitting down? she asks.

Sure, why? What's going on? I got a really strange call from —

Sibghatullah was feeling sick, she took him to the hospital. He just died.

She just says it. Quietly. Firmly. Clearly.

What? No. That can't be true! Are you sure? What do you mean, he's dead?

I hang up the phone. I cannot repeat the words. Emotions overtake me. I cannot process them, I have no tools to manage them. My body tries to dispel the feelings. First, I vomit. Then I hit my head against the wall. As a child, I once saw my mother do this when she was upset. I bang my head against the wall, pull my hair and finally understand the sound I heard in that first phone call. It is the sound of a mother having just — moments ago — lost her child.

It is the sound of anguish.

PART II

Assimilation

The story of covering my hair, my face, my entire body, including my hands, is rooted in my mother's story. And her story of covering is wrapped up in her relationship with immigration and assimilation. Like the other girls in her hometown in Pakistan, my mother started covering her hair when she was a young child. But for the first few years after immigrating, she and my dad tried to assimilate into a white Canada. My father immigrated in the sixties with a twelfth-grade education and a diploma in metallurgy. He worked in construction as a welder and pipe fitter. He 'brought' – his words, not mine – my mother to Toronto after marrying her. She was eighteen years old and bewildered by everything she saw. In the winter she was stunned by the extreme cold; in the summer she was horrified at the white bodies lounging in the sun around the swimming pool located in the centre of the apartment complex where she lived. She would peer down from her tiny apartment, dazed and disgusted by the lack of shame. She hated her tiny apartment, she always said it made her feel like an animal in a cage. She missed the courtyards and fresh air of Pakistan. She was terrified of escalators. I inherited that fear from her. To this day, my heart quickens a bit just before stepping on.

But still, under my father's influence, she tried to assimilate. They both did. Pictures of my parents from the seventies capture the people they were trying to be. My father is sometimes clean-shaven, and other times sports a fashionable trim beard. He looks a bit dodgy in his three-piece, checkered, mustard suits, and handsome in his flared pants and Ray Ban sunglasses. He poses in front of his Mustang, sometimes leaning against it, other times standing behind its open front door. My mother smiles uncertainly in bell-bottoms and a vest, with a kerchief on her head, pushing a stroller in High Park.

These pictures show two young South Asians desperately trying to fit in, to be accepted, to be white. But they were not white, they were brown. And 1970s white Canada did not let them forget it. 'Paki' is the only slur they shared with us. Even now, when they say it, I get a sense of how much it hurt them. How it took the wind out of their sails. How it made them want to give up and go back home. And they did both of those things – gave up and tried to go back home.

Many immigrants talk about the 'Dream of Return'. *One day, I'll go home. I'll make enough money to go back, back to a country I belong in, to a place that feels like home.* But the cruel fact of immigration is that once you leave, you never really have a home. You and the place you leave behind transform, ceaselessly, infinitely, so that when – if – you encounter each other again, you are unrecognisable to one another. When you visit the neighbourhood you grew up in, you wonder, *Is this the street our house was on? Or was it the next street over? Are we even in the right area?* Your relatives and friends marvel, *Is that really you? My god, I didn't recognise you!* But still, the Dream of Return remains strong; it is a dream that those immigrants cling to most desperately who do not find home in the places to which they immigrate, where they become citizens, where they pay taxes, where they have their children, where they lose their children.

I'm talking about immigration out of necessity, out of desperation. A better word for this might be 'exile', except it's not that you've been banished from your country of origin, but rather that the sorry state of the nation you're born into and your own socio-economic class leave you no choice but to try your luck elsewhere if you dare hope for a better future.

Whatever the geopolitics of the region, or the forces of the global capitalist system that led you to find yourself in this position, it does not really matter to you. All that matters is that you would rather stay home, but you know there is no hope for you there. If you want a better future, you must leave. And you must go to a wealthier nation, a nation that is privileged by the global structures of inequality. You leave because you understand the bleak future that lies ahead. And if you're really lucky, maybe you'll amass enough wealth to return home and help your parents and siblings and extended family. They'll need it, because if they stay put – as most of them will – their future will turn out even bleaker than you could have ever imagined. Poverty will destroy your family, it will ravage the bodies of your loved ones, they will fight over scraps, they will die young from preventable diseases, without access to the basic medical attention that might have saved them.

It is these immigrants that hold tight to the Dream of Return. This immigration is not the immigration of the wealthy elite of this world. It is not the immigration of those who hop nations and continents in pursuit of adventure, hobbies, an escape from boredom. Those people never actually immigrate, though in conversation they might stop and ponder with unnecessary profundity, *I guess I'm an immigrant, too!* These people don't really think of themselves as immigrants at all; they're expats. People who always belong somewhere – somewhere else – and always have the luxury to head home, their real home, anytime they so desire.

But immigrants of my parents' ilk cannot do this, they cannot just head home. They must accumulate wealth so that they can survive when they get back to a home they no longer recognise. For such immigrants, the Dream of Return remains just that, a dream that motivates them those first years and then slowly wanes and dies as they age. The Dream of Return dies for most immigrants well before they are buried in the foreign land that will become the closest thing to home that they will ever know.

My parents did not take their rejection well. They resented and bristled at the racism they experienced, at the regular insults and demands to 'go home'. So, after about a decade of trying the assimilation route, they decided to go back to Pakistan. On this front – going home – they failed, though they tried four times – no small feat with six children. Each time, they sold everything, said goodbye to their friends and adios to Canada, and relocated to Pakistan *for real this time*. Each time, their businesses flopped, they were cheated out of their money, or some such thing, and they came back to Canada to try again.

There was no possibility in their minds of remaining forever in Canada and making it their home. Under a steady barrage of racism and xenophobia, my parents gave up on trying to assimilate into Canadian society. *Fine, if you won't have us, we don't want to belong to you anyways.* Classic bitter grapes strategy. I know it is supposed to be 'sour grapes', not 'bitter grapes', but when you are born and raised in Canada speaking Urdu as your first language, you're going to mess up metaphors. And when you do, you come to expect the superior looks and condescending corrections, even when they don't make sense. I mean, 'bitter grapes' makes more sense than 'sour grapes'. Concord grapes are sour and they taste awesome. Bitter grapes makes more sense. Think about it.

Anyways, the year I was born, my mother started wearing a hijab. She retired her pants, and sewed herself some shalwar kameez. My father grew out his beard like the

Prophet's, at least one fist-length long. And they both brought their children along for the ride on this anti-assimilationist train. Surely they thought they were protecting us, saving us from the rejection that had scarred them so deeply. If we never wanted to belong in the first place, we wouldn't care when people mocked us, treated us with contempt, were unfriendly to us. My parents pulled my older brother and sister out of choir, chess club, track and all other extra-curricular activities. They got rid of the TV, stopped listening to music and quit reading anything that could be a purveyor of 'Western' culture. Instead, they focused their energies on studying Islam, learning to recite the Qur'an properly, listening to Islamic lectures from Urdu-speaking preachers on audio cassettes. If all they were going to be was 'Paki', they might as well be proper Pakis, learn their culture and their religion. Be the people they were going to get shit for being.

The way my mother tells the story, she gave up on assimilating and put on a hijab to symbolise her rejection of Canadian society and her decision to choose 'Islam' over 'Western' culture. I find this choice fascinating. In response to being rejected for being 'Paki', my mother decided to dress in an identifiably 'Muslim' way. Her response to racial discrimination was to hyper-emphasise her religious identity. She couldn't quite stop being 'Paki' but she could change the direction of the discrimination, shift it from being racial to religious. This gave her a sense of control over her persecution; she'd rather be hated, mocked, derided, cussed at for something she was choosing to wear, rather than something she could not change about herself.

The irony is that the style of hijab my mother chose to adopt was itself Western – influenced by her time in Canada, and her interaction with Canadian Muslims of different ethnicities, races and cultures. Her hijab was a square cloth, folded into a triangle and pinned at the chin. This hijab was not like the chadors and dupattas she grew up wearing in Pakistan.

Here's a brief catalogue of ways that women cover in Pakistan:

Chadors are rectangular, opaque, soft pieces of fabric that are draped over a woman's head. There are no pins or strings or ties on this fabric. The chador conceals fluidly, so you can use it to cover more or less of yourself, depending on the situation. Chadors come in various sizes. If you're out and about, you'd wear a large chador that might envelop your entire body, head to toe. If you're cooking at home while company is over, you might wear a smaller chador. Since chadors aren't pinned or tied, they don't stay put. They slip. You have to devote a good deal of energy and attention to keeping them on.

A dupatta is a gauzier version of a chador. It is also rectangular, on the smaller side, but it is light and airy. Though many women wear a dupatta at home and a chador outside, more 'modern' women will wear a dupatta outside rather than a chador. Dupattas can be fashionable. They often come with matching outfits.

A burqa, also relevant to this story, is the most conservative of coverings – it is specifically designed for outdoor wear, where your hands might be otherwise occupied and you cannot afford to use them to hold a chador in place or adjust it when it slips from its place. A burqa consists of a long, loose-fitted flowing gown and a headpiece that is tied at your chin or the back of the neck, with a face veil, a niqab, that is usually clicked into place with a tich button. Burqas are generally black, a sensible colour when you think of how often you'd have to wash a lighter-coloured burqa after walking through dusty streets. And if you don't have a washing machine, as is the case with the majority of Pakistanis, then a lighter-coloured burqa is a real hassle. A burqa makes it easier to carry groceries, herd children and be otherwise engaged in public activity. But it is also more concealing, so there isn't any chance of it slipping accidentally, and maybe revealing some hair or your face to someone you might be flirting with. A chador may require more consistent attention, making it cumbersome to be in public efficiently, but it has more fluidity; it can be less revealing should you so desire.

My mother had worn all three types of covering in Pakistan
– a dupatta, a chador and a burqa. And in those early years
when she was trying to assimilate in Canada, she felt deep
shame at removing all her coverings. She felt naked, 'nangi'.
She said she felt so much shame, she would rather the earth
itself open and swallow her whole than be seen nangi by her
father. And that's the thing, the key to understanding this
story: she wasn't ashamed before God so much as she was
ashamed before her dad. It's almost like they were merged for
her, her father a human stand-in for God, God personified.

My mother describes her father, my grandfather, as a
fiercely pious man. His name was Asad-ur-Rehman, 'Lion of
the Merciful', Mercy being one of the names of God. Asad-
ur-Rehman, the Lion of the Merciful, was known for living
up to his name. Legend had it that his piety was so fierce that
women who didn't normally cover themselves would at least
wear a dupatta when passing through his street, out of respect
for Asad-ur-Rehman's convictions. And his conviction was
that women ought to be modest and express their modesty by
concealing themselves. In these stories, my mother always
mentions two airline hostesses who would only wear their
dupattas when passing by my grandfather's street. In these
stories, the street became his too. She was really proud of this,
that her father commanded such respect and influence, that
women were afraid to pass through his street without covering themselves. I was proud of him too when I heard these
stories as a child. I was proud of my maternal lineage, proud
to be the granddaughter of such a fiercely pious man.

Funny thing about stories you learn as a child: they seem so self-evident, so true, so natural. Like the sky being blue or the grass being green. Why would you doubt these facts? Why would adults say anything misleading, why would they not know something? Then you grow up and realise that adulthood is a myth. We are children in ageing bodies, stumbling through life, pretending to know more than we do, acting like we have more control than we have.

It wasn't until I recounted this story about my grandfather to my partner that I realised – both from his widening eyes and from hearing the words coming out of my mouth – that, in this story, my grandfather comes across as a patriarchal, misogynistic tyrant. There had to be a reason why women covered themselves temporarily to pass by his house. He might have harassed them or shamed them. I shudder to think what he did or said that made all the women in the neighbourhood extra careful when walking down his street.

But in my mother's narrative, her father is the good guy. The guy whose piety is so great that women covered out of respect for him. Respect rather than fear. And she was terribly disappointed in herself for not covering in Canada. And when she thought about her father seeing her in her state of 'nakedness', which is what she called it even though she was completely covered except for her head and hands, she wished that the earth would swallow her rather than she see the disappointment on his face.

All this is the backstory for what follows. And the story is this: at some point, during that early assimilationist phase, while they were still trying to be 'Canadian', my parents went back to Pakistan for a visit. They had two kids at the time, my older siblings, five and three years old. My mother was around twenty-four. I wasn't born yet. She was excited about going to Pakistan, but also nervous. Although she wasn't covering in Canada, she packed a burqa in her suitcase. She figured she would take it out when they got to the airport in Lahore, and then wear it before the hours-long journey over potholed roads to her hometown, Gujranwala. Her parents were still alive and she was going to be staying with them. Her older brother would be there to pick her up from the airport.

My parents arrived in Pakistan having survived an over eighteen-hour flight from Toronto to Lahore, with a layover in Europe. The children were exhausted, hungry, crying and too hot in the summer heat. My mother was sleep deprived. The flight was delayed coming in, so her brother had been waiting for several hours already. Now, when my mother started going through her luggage to find her burqa, her brother, himself tired and hungry, dissuaded her. *What's the big deal?* he asked. *We're just going to get in the car and drive home. No one will see you.* He was anxious to hit the road and get home. Everyone was expecting them.

And just like that, my mother was dissuaded.

In her telling, she blames this on the crying children, her own fatigue, her brother's counsel, but I wonder if a part of her wanted to share this new Canadian version of herself with her family. Maybe a tiny part of her wanted her parents and siblings to meet and love this new person she was becoming. After all, she'd spent several years abroad, change was inevitable, and sometimes enviable. In Urdu, they use the word 'bahir' for 'abroad'. Literally, 'bahir' means 'outside', so that Pakistan is 'inside' and the rest of the world is 'outside'. It is a commonplace way to think of the private and the public, with the nation itself as the private sphere and world as the public sphere. Like domestic and foreign. The term 'bahir' can be used variously to convey a mixture of pride, contempt and envy. It can signify your connection to the outside world, perhaps a possibility for escape, perhaps a certain cosmopolitan sophistication, or it can be used as a put-down to describe visiting relatives who might be putting on airs.

At any rate, my mother did not put on her burqa. She did not cover her head to go home. Unlike the neighbour-hood women and the air hostesses, who covered their heads to pass by her father's house, my mother arrived at his house, after years away, head uncovered. Maybe she was unconsciously trying to push boundaries, to see if she was loved unconditionally. Perhaps it was an assertion of inde-pendence. *I don't live by your rules anymore.*

Whatever the (sub)conscious impulse for this decision, my mother managed to create the very scene she had dreaded for years. The scene where her father catches her, head uncovered, in public. The man who makes random women cover their hair just to pass by 'his' street encounters his very own daughter uncovered, nangi. Except, instead of this happening in Canada, which was impossible since my grandfather had no intention of ever visiting, my mother staged this scene in Pakistan, at my grandfather's very own house, on his very own street.

My parents arrived at my grandparents' house in Gujranwala. The car pulled into the narrow brick lane, stopping in the gully in front of my grandparents' home. The brick lane is slightly rounded, the middle higher than the sides, so water rolls off when it rains. Cars are always on a slant in the lane, motorcycles lean one way or the other, but horse carriages do just fine with their big wooden wheels on either side, taking up the whole lane. On either side of the lane is a small channel, with greenish-black water running through. Outdoor plumbing. This used to be the nice part of town, the one with plumbing and a sewer system from colonial times. It was called 'Civil Line'. My grandparents' house sits on the corner of two lanes, a typical house for the area. The first thing you encounter is its high stone walls. And the door, a large wooden door, with metal bolts. The walls and door yell *Private!*, and you never actually know what you'll find if you're allowed through, beyond the outer walls.

My parents came inside quickly and started to settle into the room that they would share with their children for the next few months. My grandfather was home when they arrived. He was expecting them. He saw my mother. He didn't say anything about the situation with the nakedness. Not yet, anyways. They exchanged pleasantries. It was already evening. They had dinner with the extended family, my mom's brothers and sisters, and their families. She is one of thirteen siblings. There were a lot of people, a lot of children, there was a lot of commotion. Then everyone started retiring for the night, either to their rooms or to their homes nearby. As things got quieter, my mother became more and more anxious. She knew her father wasn't going to let this go. He was going to, at the very least, say something. She wished she could just say something herself and get the anticipation over with, but she was too frightened, she didn't have the courage.

Finally, she retired to her room. The lights started to turn off. My mother's room had a window that opened on to the courtyard of this large house. Courtyards make cloistered spaces more friendly for women. They can enjoy the outdoors, the winter sun, the monsoon rains, without leaving the house. In the courtyard tonight, my mother watched her father pace back and forth, smoking cigarettes. She heard his slow, measured footsteps, watched the red burning tobacco, as he paced steadily, deliberately, from one end of the courtyard to the other and back.

She knew he was going to say something to her. What would he say? She hoped he wouldn't be cruel and humiliate her in front of her husband and children. She didn't want him to do her 'bay-izzati'. 'Izzat' means 'honour' or 'dignity'. When someone does your bay-izzati, they rob you of your honour, your dignity. What if he yelled and screamed and kicked them out of his house? She made calculations in her mind: where would she go? One of her sisters' places? Their husbands might not be inclined to host a family of four to whom they had no patrilineal obligation. One of her brothers' places? Most were too poor to host them.

She followed the red embers of the cigarette as it moved back and forth across the courtyard, my grandfather's face obscured in the dark. Finally, he walked toward her room, opened the door and walked in. My mother was ready for him, sitting on the chaar-pai.

If you're wondering where my dad is in this story, you raise a good point. In telling this story, my mother barely mentions him. Is he sitting with her, anxiously wondering what will happen next? After all, his fate is tied to hers. If her father throws them out, he will have to fend for the family. The tension between my mother and her own father is so intense in this moment that it erases everyone else. Her husband and children are no longer. All that remains is the bond between father and daughter. Will it survive this moment?

And the fact that my grandfather can just walk into their room – a grown, married couple with children, after bedtime – is an expression of power and entitlement. This is, after all, his house. He may go where he pleases. He's not worried about etiquette. My parents are guests in his house, they are at his mercy. He can let them stay or throw them out. He can tell them what to do, what to wear. His opinion matters. His feelings matter.

My mother is half relieved and half terrified that the moment she has been dreading is finally here. My grandfather sits across from my mother, avoids eye contact, looks away from her, looks at the floor. He speaks quietly.

Did I see correctly that you arrived at my house with your head naked?

Yes, she whispers.

He nods his head thoughtfully, slowly.

I wondered if I'd seen correctly, if perhaps my eyes were lying to me.

She is silent. He continues.

I thought it can't be, that my own Baby would come to my home with a nanga head.

That is actually my mother's nickname. Not Urdu for 'baby', but the English word itself. Colonialism made English the official language of Pakistan, alongside Urdu.

Not when the neighbourhood women wouldn't dare walk by my house with naked heads. Baby wouldn't come to my house with a naked head.

I'm sorry, Abba-ji. I didn't mean to disrespect you. I wanted to unpack the burqa at the airport but Bhai said not to worry about it.

She blamed her brother. In doing so she admits that she doesn't wear a burqa in Canada, and was planning to take it out at the airport. Her father doesn't seem to care. He's fixated on her not wearing it around him, not wearing it when she comes to *his* house, *his* street. This is about him. His reputation.

Your brother is a son of a bitch. You shouldn't have listened to him. Do you cover for him or for Allah?

Even though he says she should cover for God, he means himself. And it is from him that she asks forgiveness.

I'm sorry, Abba-ji. I made a mistake, please forgive me.

He does forgive her, but not without shaming her. He speaks the words she has expected to hear for years, the words she believes she deserves to hear, the words she's dreaded since the day she stopped covering her hair. The words she did not want to hear so badly, she wished the ground would swallow her up instead. But also the words she gave her father the chance to utter, by somehow not covering her head when she came to visit, becoming – as we sometimes do – the architect of her own nightmare.

He said, *The neighbourhood that would rather cover its women than have them pass by the house of Asad-ur-Rehman with naked heads, today that neighbourhood saw my own daughter disembark from a car and enter the threshold of my house with her head naked. You have made a mockery of me. Today, you made me hang my head in shame. I will not be able to raise it again.*

Then he left and never brought up the conversation again.

And my mother saw him for only a few more years, with her head always covered. By the time he died, she was burqa-clad in Canada.

It would be easy to say that this encounter between daughter and father, between my mother and my grandfather, is the reason my mother eventually donned a burqa in Canada. But the truth is far more complicated than that. Remember, my grandfather was only upset that my mother came to his threshold, his house, his neighborhood, without her burqa. He didn't care what she wore in Canada.

The story between my mother and her father, that's a script we're familiar with, we've heard this story before. Muslim patriarchy suffocating Muslim women. But this story is bigger than that. The reason, in the end, that my mother decided to wear a burqa in Canada was not because of Muslim patriarchy, but because of racism, because of a decade spent trying to assimilate but failing – and it felt like failure – to be accepted as Canadian.

When my mother donned a burqa in Canada, years after this incident with her father, it was as a shield from racism. It was racism that would eventually make fundamentalist Islam appealing to her. Wearing a niqab did not increase the persecution and discrimination my mother faced. But now, instead of the insults, the cruel words and harsh looks hurting her feelings – *Why do you hate me because of my colour?* – my mother could believe that her persecution was a measure of her sincerity, her worthiness. Enduring religious persecution is noble, honourable, principled, meritorious; it is heroic. To be persecuted for your beliefs and to remain steadfast in the face of persecution, that is the stuff of legend.

And this is how it came to be that I was born into a house filled with the religious zeal of new converts, and why I began wearing a hijab when I was young. So young as to not remember when I started. Raised in the cradle of a religious identity fashioned as a shield, a protection from racism.

Second Generation

I started wearing hijab before consciousness, before I have any memory of putting it on. It is as if I emerged into being with my head already covered. I only know how I came to wear hijab from stories my mother tells. She tells me that I started wearing it when I was five years old. She's really proud of this. She says she didn't force me to wear it; on the contrary, I had insisted. I was a strong-willed child. I didn't like 'no' as an answer. I still don't. Does anyone?

My mother herself started wearing hijab the year I was born. By the time I started kindergarten, I asked if I could wear hijab too. My mother tried to dissuade me.

You're too young. When you're older you can wear it for sure.

But I want to wear it now!

You're too young, what will people say? They'll think I'm forcing you!

She tells me that I started stealing her hijabs, wearing them to school and then coming home, dragging them behind me, all muddy and dirty. Her hijabs were too big for my tiny body. After enough ruined hijabs, she relented and sewed me some my size; square fabric, which you folded into a triangle and then pinned at your chin, but really your throat, with a safety pin. At that age, I doubt my mother pinned the hijab at my throat. She probably just tied it under my chin, like a kerchief that elderly Eastern European women wear on their heads sometimes. I would graduate to the safety pin.

My earliest memory of wearing hijab is having forgotten to wear it. I was attending the Islamic School in Toronto. There were Muslims from all over the world at this school. The Sudanese principal had a thin, white metal rod, four feet long, that he carried around the school with him. He would use it to discipline misbehaving children, sometimes with a sharp, stinging strike to their hands. He believed in public punishment so that the other children would know what to expect if they misbehaved. I saw him hit a young boy once. The child shrieked, his face crumpling with pain and shame, reddening, his eyes squinting as he hopped frantically from one foot to the other. I feel I was hit by this rod too. I have a vivid memory of how it felt on my hand. I say 'feel' because I'm not sure if I've conjured up this experience with my elaborate childhood imagination. Maybe I was hit and I blocked out the details. Or maybe I spent so much time and emotional energy terrified, imagining how it would feel to be hit by the rod, that I imagined that it happened. Either way, we were all terrified of the principal's rod. Terror is only effective when it takes hold of our imagination.

But the principal was also very nice to me. One evening after a fundraising event, when people milled about after dinner in a sparse and cavernous community hall, with walls painted white, the floor a beige linoleum and lights fluorescent and bright, I remember he played with me, lifting me off the floor and twirling me around. I loved the attention. He asked my parents if he could adopt me for a few years. He promised to teach me flawless Arabic.

Your daughter is special, he told them. *She could be a great scholar.*

There were Canadians from all over the world at the Islamic School: South Asians from India and Pakistan; Arabs from Saudi, Syria and Egypt; converts, European and Japanese. Everyone came with their own cultural background, their own vision of a pristine Islam. All these visions jostled with one another to create a mosaic, an Islamic mosaic, at this school.

But my parents didn't think Islam should be a mosaic. They didn't like the way Islam was being practised there – it was too diluted, too weak, too Western. There was too much mixing between the genders. Why did this school have co-ed classes? Did they care nothing for Islam? Qur'an memorisation, or lack thereof, was a particular sore point for my parents. I'd learned to recite the Qur'an very early, and had read it in its entirety by the time I was five years old. The Qur'an is divided into siparas, thirty sections of roughly equal length. I had memorised the last sipara in its entirety by the time I was seven, and my parents expected me to keep pace with memorisation at the Islamic School. But my peers were still only just learning to recite the Qur'an, and they were way behind me on the memorisation. And to make matters worse, the Islamic School was an hour-long bus ride away, and the long commute meant less time to keep up with my memorisation when I got home. So what was the point of sending me to Islamic school if I wasn't learning anything Islamic, not even the Qur'an?

I wonder if my parents also pulled me out of the Islamic School because they couldn't afford to pay the fees. How were they going to send all six children there? Whatever the reason, by third grade, I was back in public school.

But while in Islamic school, one winter morning, in between grabbing my lunch, pulling on my jacket, leg warmers, gloves and hat, I forgot to also wear my hijab. I didn't realise this until I was on my way to school. As I warmed up on the bus, I went to remove my hat and discovered, with horror and shame, that I'd forgotten to wear my hijab! The realisation knocked the breath out of me. I froze. My ears started ringing. I quickly replaced the hat on my head, looked around guiltily to make sure no one had seen my hair and tried to disappear into the bus seat. At school I whispered what had happened to my teacher, Sister Nobuko.

Something really bad has happened. I trembled, *I forgot my hijab.*

To my surprise, she was nonchalant. *Oh, well, you don't have to wear it today.*

What? Had she lost her mind? I was a Muslim girl, I had to wear hijab. You couldn't just not wear it. I felt naked without my hijab. Like I'd forgotten to wear pants and everyone was just rolling with it. *Oh well, that happens sometimes. Spend the day without pants and tomorrow you can remember to wear them.* What the fuck?

Sister Nobuko saw that I was going to have trouble participating in class, because I stood frozen in place, looking at the floor in shame. She took an exasperated sigh and said, *Well, we can grab one from the bin of extra hijabs we keep for prayer time. Would you like one of those?*

I gratefully accepted this offer, taking the hijab from her hands with a mixture of urgency and relief. I don't know the last time that hijab had been washed. The smell of many heads mingled in the scent of the hijab to create a pungent, spicy perfume. I didn't care. I'd rather wear a dodgy-smelling hijab than walk shamelessly with my head uncovered all day. As relief washed over me, energy returned to my body. I stood taller, uncrumpling myself. Once again, I felt comfortable at school; I was chatty and enthusiastic. I added my own scent of oiled, thick Pakistani hair to that hijab.

Once I started public school, hijab moved from being a personal expression of my religious conviction to a central part of my identity. At the Islamic School, no one was hung up on my hijab, but in public school, it became the first and sometimes the only thing people saw of me. It's like they had this reductive, simplistic idea of the hijab and Muslims, and they just projected that on to me. They couldn't even see me. They didn't see my adorable face, or my oversized eye glasses. (I always wanted the biggest glasses – they made me feel like an adult, and this was the eighties.) They didn't notice my outgoing, chatty, even spunky personality. Instead, they noticed and commented on my hijab. Even though I didn't spend every waking moment thinking about it – it was just something I wore, and like all regularly worn things I forgot I was wearing it – no one else could get over it.

Why are you wearing that? they'd ask.

Where are you from?

Is that from your religion?

What would happen if I saw your hair?

Do you wear it when you sleep?

Do you wear that in the shower?

Aren't you too hot?

Who made you wear it? Your parents? Like their parents didn't make them wear the clothes they were wearing.

The questions were ceaseless and incessant. Sometimes they were asked out of curiosity, other times pity, moral judgement, suspicion. The questions always betrayed the privilege of the questioner. To feel that you have the right to walk up to a stranger and ask them why they are wearing what they are wearing, this comfort lies with those who do not have to ask themselves the same questions. Always, the questions made me feel like an outsider, like I didn't belong, demanded that I explain myself, justify my very existence.

Canada is a cultural mosaic, we were taught in our curriculum. *As a country of immigrants, we value everyone's cultural and religious contributions. You don't have to leave your culture and religion behind to belong here; we accept all of you. Your cultural and religious characteristics are small, colourful tiles; each one adds to the beauty of the larger mosaic that is Canada.*

But some cultures and religions belonged more than others. Some clothes were more 'Canadian' than others. The hijab hadn't, and still hasn't, made it into the cultural mosaic.

I became good at answering the questions, they were so frequent, so predictable, so . . . boring. Like everyone was working with the same script, asking the same questions over and over and over again. I was so much more than my hijab. I had ideas about things. But most people couldn't get past the fabric on my head to hear me. Not my classmates, not my teachers, not strangers in the supermarket. I'd answer patiently, calmly, mindlessly. Other times, my answers were testy, frustrated, annoyed.

I wear this because of my religion. I am a Muslim.

Nothing would happen if you saw my hair.

No, I don't wear it to sleep.

No, I don't wear it in the shower. How would that even work?!

No, I'm not too hot. And it's hotter in Hell.

I'm from here! I was born in Canada.

And then, in my head, *This is what a Canadian looks like, motherfuckers.*

I felt so defiant and self-righteous saying this, even just in my head. I relished sullying what was clearly pure and pristine in their minds, by turning the pollution into the thing itself. This was not the first time my body was cast as a pollutant, tainting, spoiling what is pure. In some, but not all, Islamic legal texts, women's bodies are seen as polluting to communal rituals and sacred spaces; and here was my body cast as a pollutant again, but this time defiling the idea of a Canadian. The people who saw me as an outsider had an idea of what a 'Canadian' looked like, they saw themselves reflected in this idea, this idea was precious to them. I did not fit in their vision, in their self-image; my existence corrupted their vision. But what if I were the vision itself? What if I could ruin how they looked at themselves? Ruin their self-image.

What I did not understand then is that my desire to be 'Canadian', to be accepted as such, was shaped by fear. In claiming the identity of a 'Canadian', I was holding on to the very thing that was being used to reject me. I was looking for stability in the thing that was creating precariousness for me to begin with – citizenship. But what does it mean, really, to 'look' Canadian, to 'be' Canadian? What does it mean for me to claim this identity as a South Asian woman, a progeny of a double diaspora, displaced by colonialism and into a settler colonial state?

Any joy I might squeeze from this petty rejoinder was short-lived. For to say the sentence itself, to claim 'Canadianness' at all, is to already be ensnared by the logic of the state.

The state artificially creates the conditions of its own citizenship, in which some are embraced while others are rejected. It draws a line around itself, telling all outside the line that it owes them nothing, and demands that all inside the line become subjects of the state, whether they like it or not. It represents itself as the solution to the very problems it creates.

In claiming citizenship, I was begging to inherit the sins of the state. The genocides, the war crimes, the selling of arms to dictators, the structural racism, the institutionalised patriarchy. Blind patriotism demands a great deal of forgetting and selective remembering. It requires a whitewashing of history, so we can feel virtuous as we kill and oppress and dispossess in the name of the nation. We forget, no, we erase the sins so we can celebrate ourselves simply, which requires us to first craft simplistic stories about ourselves. If erasing our sins means erasing entire peoples and histories, including our own, so be it. We demand this forgetting, this erasure, as the cost of 'good citizenship', and we are angry, frustrated, annoyed when people refuse to participate in the erasure, when they insist on reminding us of our sins, when they insist on remembering.

By its very existence, the Canadian state displaces and alienates those who are indigenous to the land it lays claim over; it demands they justify their right to continue existing on land they are already living on, and defend that right to foreign, unwelcome colonisers. In other words, the state creates a hell from which citizenship to this same state becomes the only respite, maybe the only reprieve. What I'm saying is, by making citizenship a form of belonging, the state turns itself into a refuge from itself. And this is how God describes Herself in the Qur'an:

لا ملجأ من الله إلا إليه

There is no refuge from God except in God.

When the state turns itself into a refuge from itself, the state turns itself into a god. Worshipping a god that is not God is a sin called 'shirk'. Shirk is the only unforgivable sin in Islam.

Theft

When I was little, say maybe four or five years old, I joined my mother on a visit to her friend's house. We didn't grow up wealthy. My mother managed our home, produced and raised six children. She did this mostly alone, because my father worked long hours and was often at work when we were awake. When I was young, we lived in rental apartments, and whenever we had to move and my parents had to find a new apartment to rent, they would leave us with friends. They would hide the fact that they had so many children. They would hope that the landlord would not ask them how many children they had, so that they wouldn't have to lie. But they lied when necessary. Most landlords would balk at the idea of three, four, five, and eventually six children living in a small space. It was difficult to explain to them that we weren't spoiled and undisciplined, like gora children. We were South Asian and Muslim, and unable to afford living in large houses; we weren't going to be allowed to misbehave, run wild and destroy our chances of living somewhere.

At the time of this visit, when I accompanied my mother to her friend's house, we were living in a small apartment in Toronto, four children in a two-bedroom apartment. We didn't have a lot of furniture. We had a couch for entertaining, a kitchen table and chairs, but we didn't have beds. My parents thought wall-to-wall carpeting was amazing. Who needed beds? Just throw down a sheet and pillow and you're set! Plus, beds were expensive and took up a lot of space. What was the point? My father worked as a pipe fitter and a welder. He sent extra money back home to Pakistan to support extended family on both sides, and Islamic causes. We were fortunate to have so much.

But when we visited other people, I saw how little we had. Other people had fancy bedroom furniture, dressers, side tables, elegant beds. Some girls had princess beds with a canopy! Oh, how I envied these children. They had TVs, they could watch movies. My mother's friend even had a cabinet full of only decorative stuff! She had little crystal figurines in it, like a bird or a bear, and I watched the light create dazzling colours as it filtered through the crystal. I could see purples and pinks and greens. I became mesmerised and obsessed with one figurine of a bird, its wings just spread for flight. It was so elegant, so beautiful, so bewitching. I touched it; it was stunning. I couldn't part with it. Before we left this aunty's house, I pocketed it. She had other beautiful things. She wouldn't miss it. And I *needed* to have it. So, I stole it. Except, I was too young to understand the concept of theft.

But the adults understood. Her friend called our home later that night and told my mother that the figurine was missing. My mother assured her that she would deal with it. And she did. By teaching me about stealing, which is taking something that belongs to someone else without their consent. Apparently, it didn't matter how much you liked it or needed it.

When my parents consulted with one another and considered how they would teach me about stealing, the conversation portion of the lesson wasn't immediately followed by a lesson on forgiveness, where I return the figurine to its owner, apologise and am forgiven. That *did* happen. Eventually. But first, there was a theatrical detour.

In Islam, my parents taught me, *if you steal, your hand gets chopped off.*

And since I had stolen, I deserved to have my hand chopped off. My father was to do the deed.

And this is how it came to pass that I remember crouching behind the couch we used for entertaining, squeezed between the wall and the back of the couch, terrified, looking up, as I see my father peering down at me, brandishing an axe. Or at least that is what I've believed my entire life, until recently, when recounting this story to a group of friends, they convinced me that it was, more likely, a hatchet. Obviously, I didn't know the difference. I was crying, and at some point my mother pulled me out, hugged and consoled me, assured me that though I'd narrowly escaped punishment this time, there were no guarantees next time. Better not steal again.

I think my parents were proud of themselves for doing such a great job teaching me a valuable lesson. It wouldn't do to have their children stealing. This was serious. You couldn't fuck with the law. They were uncertain of how they'd help me if I got in trouble with the law, if I got in the habit of stealing. Better nip this in the bud.

In his book *Between the World and Me*, Ta-Nehisi Coates talks about how his parents beat him out of fear for what might happen to him in the streets, at the hands of white authorities. The beating was meant to be a kind of protection, a kind of love. It seems they believed that the violence they employed to educate Coates would serve him well, especially if it saved him from violence beyond the house. As long as they were doing the hitting, they were in control of it. They loved him. So they wouldn't hurt him irrevocably. He wouldn't die at their hands. In this way, violence becomes a teaching, a kindness, a mercy even.

My mother always says, محبت کی مار مکھن سے بھی نرم ہے

A beating from love – a *'love-beating'*, perhaps – *is softer than butter.*

Maybe Coates's parents figured that there was some algorithm that determined the amount of violence in the world, like we were all owed a portion of it, and if they administered it themselves, they could control it, be measured and merciful with their son's quota. Because they couldn't trust the authorities, the state, to be measured or merciful. The state and its apparatus are monstrous, murderous, careless, merciless with bodies of colour, especially with black bodies. Or maybe they thought a certain level of violence was necessary to keep him in line, so that he might never encounter the authorities. Which feeds the myth that the 'authorities' are only ever involved when we step out of line. Or maybe . . . or maybe . . . or maybe . . .

This is what the state does to the populations it marginalises – it dominates us with such ferocity, the mere threat of its violence is so terrifying, it fools us into imagining that our controlled violence against our own, against ourselves, will spare us greater, more fearsome violence. And so, the state comes to appear benevolent in the face of our own monstrosities. And we hurt the ones we love, in the name of love. And protection. Through violence.

I have only two memories of my grandfather, both from family trips to Pakistan. In one, he's in a bed in one of the rooms in my mamoo's portion of the house. The room is painted a light shade of green. It is a house that my grandfather claimed after Partition. He fled to Pakistan from India with his family, leaving behind farmlands, cattle and a haveli, a compound of houses – immovable wealth. Apparently, the way it worked during Partition was that if you survived the massacres in your home town, escaped the knives of your neighbours, jewellers, butchers and school teachers, once-friends now turned enemies based on lines drawn by white men over lunches in posh rooms; if you survived the violence along the way, on the roads and train stations, stations turned – for a little while – into battlefields and slaughterhouses, running red with rivers of blood; if you finally made it to the place where you were supposed to be, which wasn't your home because that had been left behind, but the place where it had been decided by the people who would never be called thieves that you'd have to start your life over, then what you would do is find an empty house, another displaced family's home, and move into it and claim it as your own. Finders keepers following partition, displacement and massacre.

The house my grandparents settled into is a large home that used to belong to a Punjabi Hindu or Sikh family; we know this because it was abandoned. My grandfather claimed it. Growing up, I heard this was a wealthy family's house, evidenced by the fact that they left behind an entire trunk full of chocolates. Now the house is partitioned in two as my grandfather lies weak, ill and dying, surrounded by his children and grandchildren in a room in a part of the house that two of his seven sons live in. The other half is occupied by another son. The sons split the house in two, and the partition was not amicable. The brothers fought over portions of the house, each feeling cheated out of his fair share. And the three who claimed the house, two in one section and one in the other, screwed their remaining siblings – including my mother – out of their rightful claim over a house the family barely had a claim over to begin with.

I'm not sure how old I am in this scene, maybe I'm five. The white-bearded, light-skinned, frail man on the bed, my grandfather, is dying. Some people are weeping, speaking in hushed tones. There is a sense of great importance in the room; something is about to happen. I'm not there when it does. I am told that just before he died, he smelled blossoms, asking, *Where are all these flowers coming from?* There were no flowers in the room. This is a good sign. The smell of flowers means he is headed to Jannah, the Garden, Paradise, encountering its smell before its sight. He smelled Heaven while still alive, in the liminal space between life and death, when he could still communicate, when he could still tell us, *There are flowers in Paradise! I smell them!*

The next time I see him, he is dead. His washed body lying on a chaar-pai. There is a huge slab of ice the size of a coffin underneath the chaar-pai, cooling the body from below so it doesn't rot. The body, the chaar-pai, the coffin-sized block of ice are all in the courtyard of the house. I think it is summer, and early evening, so likely about 7:00P.M. Some of the adults are wailing. My mother's sister brings me close to the body.

Go ahead, look at him. He's your nana.

Your grandfather. Your mother's father. The words for maternal and paternal grandfather are different in Urdu, 'nana' and 'dada', respectively. The difference between these grandfathers is significant. You have different claims over each. They have different kinds of power over you.

Go ahead, look at him. He's your nana.

Even now, as I remember or manufacture this scene, I am aware that she means to convey something important to me, but I don't get it. Not then, not now. What is she trying to tell me? Maybe she wants me to know where I'm from, my maternal lineage. Maybe she's just overcome with grief and this encounter has nothing to do with me. That's more likely; this is about her. But I don't know that when I'm five. And more than thirty years later, I remember that exchange, but I doubt she has any recollection of it.

I go into a dark back room off the courtyard, crossing into another section of the house, and hang out with my cousins, who are also children. We discuss, try to process what has just happened, and how we should behave.

Our grandfather just died, says one cousin.

We should be sad, says another.

Let's cry, suggests a third.

Good idea, we agree.

So we try to make ourselves cry, mimicking the adults, forcing feelings of sadness I don't actually feel. After all, I never had a relationship with this man who has just died, this man named Asad-ur-Rehman. Beautiful name when you think about it. Not the 'Lion of God', but the 'Lion of the Merciful'. A name that holds opposites, that imagines fierceness and mercy together, at once.

As I think back on this strange memory of being in a dark room that feels like a cave, the walls made of stone and brick, moisture seeping through them so the room feels damp, pretending to be sad, fake crying at the death of a grandfather I never knew, I wonder, is this the first memory I have of feeling like a fraud? I wonder too, can grief be stolen? What I'm really asking is, can grief be owned?

There is a contested story about the British East India Company involving the thumbs of Bengali weavers. According to oral accounts, the thumbs of Bengali weavers were cut off by the British to prevent them from competing with the East India Company in the textile trade. But a written account, by a colonialist himself, states that the East India Company's labour practices were so horrific that Bengali weavers cut off their own thumbs rather than allow their labour to be stolen by the British. Where does the truth of the missing thumbs lie, in the oral history of Indigenous peoples or the written history of colonisers? Memories, too, it turns out, can be stolen.

In the episode with the hatchet, I was never physically hurt. The mere threat of violence was enough to put the fear of God in me. The fear of God can be more merciful than the fear of the state. God can be shaped and reshaped by us, but we are helpless before the state.

And it worked. I learned the lesson I was supposed to. That people and things can be owned. That some people own more things than others. That ownership is virtuous and, even more, it is a protected right. Taking something that someone else claims ownership over is called 'theft'. It does not matter how little you have, or how much they have, or how they came by what they have, taking it is a crime and a sin. The crime is both moral and legal. Laws – religious and secular – punish the thief. The punishment is often physical, whether it involves cutting off a hand, or confining you to a cage, stealing years from your life.

I learned this lesson living on stolen land, land stolen by Europeans from the Indigenous peoples whom they mistook as 'Indians' and then called 'Indians' anyways. Stealing their identities, their names, their land, their kin, their children, their language. Teaching us that what is not owned can still be stolen.

So the lesson I learned was this: the powerless have only a merciful God to rely upon, whereas the powerful can rely on the mercy of the state.

Unexpected Visitors

Whenever I hear about incredible, selfless people who devote their lives to the service of others, who sacrifice their own needs so they may help others in need, I wonder about the ways they fail their own families to be these people. It's not that I don't admire them, that I'm not impressed by their sacrifices. It's just that I know that the 'self' in 'self-sacrifice' more often than not includes the sacrifice of other 'selves', the selves in one's family, those known as 'loved ones'. These people – one's own partners, children, siblings, parents – don't count in the category of 'others', the 'others' whom one helps. So, when I hear about Mother Teresa, I wonder about her family. What did they think of her? What did she do for them? What did they give up? Same thing with Martin Luther King, Jr., Gandhi, even Jesus.

Here, I'm reminded of that passage from the New Testament, where Jesus is with the believers, preaching to the crowds. He's having a moment with his congregants, and suddenly, this moment is interrupted by an announcement.

Your mother and brothers are standing outside, wanting to speak with you.

How long have they been there, waiting outside, waiting to be let in, to see Jesus, to speak to him, waiting for his permission? Why are they even waiting outside? Why haven't they just come in expecting to be welcomed? Are they being kept outside by a guard, or some equivalent of a bouncer?

I expect Jesus to jump up and run outside, to greet his family, to apologise for their wait, to say, *Yes, yes, of course, let them in!*

But he doesn't do that. Instead, he responds in a way that strikes me as rude, insulting even. Instead of responding with a gesture of welcome and respect, he rejects his family's claim over him while paradoxically expanding the notion of kinship itself.

Who is my mother, and who are my brothers? he asks.

His question is a spurning, a turning away. His question makes a stranger of his mother, the woman who carried him in her womb for nine months, who nourished him from her body, providing him nutrients by draining them from her own bones, then suckled him, cared for him, bore ostracism because of him. How can she make a claim over him if he doesn't even recognise their relationship?

Then Jesus points to those around him, to the disciples, to the crowds, people whom he has known for years, and people whom he met only months ago, weeks and days ago, maybe even moments ago. There are people in the crowds whom Jesus has never met before, he does not even know their names. Yet he says, *Here are my mother and my brothers. For whoever does the will of my Father in Heaven is my brother and sister and mother.*

I found myself studying this text with some Christian theologians at Cambridge University, and they insisted that this passage was about the radical inclusion of Christianity. That in this sentence, Jesus' family, his mothers and his brothers and his sisters, are multiplied manifold. His sense of obligation to family is expanded to include strangers. *How benevolent!* they said, wanting me to see the generosity, the magnanimity of Christ.

But I found myself standing outside with Jesus' mother and his brothers. What did his words mean to them? How did they receive them? How much pain did it cause them? Are they let in, or are they turned away after this little lesson about how unspecial they are and how special everyone else is? And how special is family if it can be undone so easily, so lightly? Would you want to be the mother or brother of a man who so easily disowns his own?

My Christian theologian friends had a point: it is great to have an expansive notion of kinship. But they could not see, or would not see, that in this case, expansion is achieved through exclusion, by making expendable Jesus' mother and brothers. Sure, in saying, *Here are my mother and my brothers*, Jesus' mother and brothers are indeed multiplied manifold. But this sentence comes in response to a question posed by Jesus, *Who is my mother, and who are my brothers?* And this question is a misrecognition; it excludes his sense of obligation to his blood kin in service of the kinship of faith that he is trying to create.

Each person only has a limited amount of energy. When we spend our time and energy on some, we neglect others. It's always a trade-off. Self-sacrifice for others comes at the expense of family. They are a part of the self that is perhaps too easily sacrificed.

In my family, we did not celebrate birthdays. When you grow up in a religiously zealous household, religious reasoning is used to explain, justify, a lot of things. Many of these things may not be about religion at the start. It may be that your family does something because of pragmatic financial reasons, but then, once it has been explained and justified using religious reasoning, it becomes infused with virtue and piety, taking on a life of its own.

I don't know exactly why my parents decided not to celebrate birthdays. There could be many reasons. For one thing, it is not a very South Asian thing to do. I mean, South Asians do celebrate birthdays now, but that is more a function of globalisation than of South Asian culture. South Asian Muslims have a long tradition of celebrating the birthdays (and death days) of important people, like the Prophet Muhammad, but not necessarily the birthdays of family members. Also, in a continent where birthdays weren't even recorded until recently, birthday celebrations don't make a lot of sense. And this isn't in the ancient past either. We don't know what day, month or even year my father was born – he believes he was born in 1942 or 1944. When my father was applying for a Canadian visa, he just made up his birth date, picking the first day of a month. His first daughter and second child would later be born on that very same day. Now they share a birthday, but his is made up.

It's always interesting to me when my white friends talk about their genealogies, how they can trace their family tree back several generations to so-and-so, how they have written records of their ancestors. I can't do that, because I don't have written records dating back even two generations. This is the result of being born to a people whose culture isn't obsessed with writing and bureaucracy. That is the easy and bullshit and racist way to explain it. But really, it is the result of belonging to a people ravaged by colonialism, by a colonialism where white people kept a record of themselves in India, but didn't think to record details – and outright destroyed records – of a people they considered on a par with dogs. British colonialism in South Asia is a story soaked in barbarity and inhumanity dressed up as civilisation. Formal British colonialism ended with genocide, resulting in the mass migration and displacement, forced expulsion, of my parents' generation. Millions of people were displaced, forcibly moved between India and Pakistan. That this genocidally motivated expulsion is called 'migration' in popular historical narratives demonstrates how violence is sanitised and experiences of entire peoples erased to keep the powerful from taking responsibility for their crimes.

When running from their homes, as news arrived of violence close at hand, because they belonged to the wrong religion and lived in the wrong place, my grandparents couldn't be burdened with tomes of paper when they needed to be light and quick. They could only take with them what they could literally carry. Maybe they thought they would return home later and collect their belongings, their lives, left behind at a moment's notice. But it turned out they were lucky just to have survived. They would never see home again. For the rest of their lives, they'd carry instead the loss of home, the loss of a sense of belonging, dreams of the past, a place where they were born, had lived for generations, a home abandoned to memory. And their records, hastily left behind, were likely destroyed by the families that replaced them in their homes, who put down roots for a new future, a new start, a new story of a different family.

Birthdays are also very expensive, what with all the presents and cakes. If you have six children, the dollars add up. And if you want to throw a party, then you have to go to other children's birthday parties too. Suddenly, you're buying presents for dozens of children every year. So it makes sense that my immigrant parents, who lived with six children on a single blue-collar income, might have decided not to celebrate birthdays due to financial constraints. But that's embarrassing. It's hard to tell your kids you can't afford to celebrate their birthdays in a culture where birthday celebrations are normal. And how do you explain to them that they are also not allowed to celebrate their friends' birthdays, that they must decline invitations to their birthday parties, that you can't buy them presents?

What if there was a way to feel good, righteous, about not celebrating birthdays? Ah, but there is: religion! Instead of telling us that celebrating birthdays was really expensive and that they couldn't afford the ritual, or that celebrating birthdays was a culturally strange ritual for them, this is what my parents, god bless them, said to us:

We don't celebrate birthdays because we are Muslim and Muslims don't celebrate birthdays. What is there to celebrate anyways? You're a year closer to death and what do you have to show for it? Muhammad bin Qasim conquered India at the age of eighteen, what have you done?

When I was young, I bought into this. Why *did* people celebrate birthdays? What was the point? We *were* a year closer to death every year. As morbid as that thought was, it was true. And, truth be told, I was insecure about Muhammad bin Qasim. How did he conquer India when he was so young? Why was I so unaccomplished compared to him? My concerns seemed petty compared to his. I worried about exams and papers, while he brought glory to Islam and Muslims. Why couldn't I be more like him?

Only later would I understand the importance of perspective in experiencing the grandness of life. As in the case of the half-filled glass, where you can focus on it being half empty or half full, birthdays could be an opportunity to reflect – with gratitude – on the days enjoyed on Earth, or a moment to consider – with sorrow and regret – the loss of yet another year in the ceaseless passage of time. And it would be a while still before I learned about privilege, how Muhammad bin Qasim was a privileged male, son of a governor, and that he probably had little to do with earning the credentials to lead an army to conquer any place. Likely, his bloodline, birth order and genitals determined this role for him. And that the conquest of India, as with any conquest ever, was a nasty event, involving the death and displacement of countless and forever unremembered and unrecorded people.

Growing up, our house was always filled with people. Not just our ever-expanding family of six children, then their spouses, then their children, but also people unrelated to us, strangers. My parents' commitment to anti-assimilation meant that they tried to keep us at home as much as possible. If we were away from home, they could not watch and control us. Who knows, we might watch TV if we visited a friend in their home, cavort with the opposite sex if the homes weren't gender segregated, which they never were. Who knows what shenanigans we might get up to; we might go to the mall, go outside, unsupervised. So, as a rule, we weren't allowed to visit friends' homes or play with them outside. They had to come over to our TV-less, music-less, novel-less, mostly toy-less home if they wanted to hang out. But since there was little to do at our place, you can imagine that our house wasn't a prime destination. Still, if we were working on a project, friends might come over. Or they might stop by to just hang out and talk.

Mostly, the visitors were my parents' friends and their kids. But my parents also welcomed strangers who were going through a transition period and needed a place to live for a few weeks or months as they immigrated to Canada, or a husband who went to work in the United States and his pregnant wife waited for her visa to arrive, or families that wanted to spend a weekend away from their own home, or families who had moved away but were in town visiting friends, people connected to my parents through friends, or friends of friends. Sometimes the visitors arranged their visit beforehand, they showed up according to plan on a certain date and time; other times they dropped by unannounced and unexpected.

My mother loved unannounced and unexpected visitors. For her, these people recreated the feeling of growing up in post-Partition Pakistan, when people didn't call ahead before stopping by for a visit. Not everyone had phones back then, so there might have been a technological barrier for calling ahead. But even after phones became accessible and widely available, people persisted in unannounced visits. In the cloistered lives of women in my mother's family, who needed a legitimate excuse and permission to leave the house, these kinds of visitors were delightful. I suppose that as a homemaker with six children, the primary place my mother socialised was in private spaces – her own home and her friends' homes and, of course, the masjid. The fact that the masjid was a place for my mother to socialise was a unique feature of her life in Canada, since most masjids in Pakistan architecturally exclude women.

Having a friend drop by unexpectedly was akin to running into someone on the sidewalk or subway and having a pleasant conversation. It broke the monotony of the day. It added a new challenge. And somehow, my mother managed to find a whole group of people in Canada who were also nostalgic for the freedom to drop by unannounced, unexpected. This community relished the comfort and freedom of just showing up to someone's house and expecting to be hosted graciously. The unwitting hosts don't complain; on the contrary, they're thrilled to see you, they see it as a compliment and an honour, a sign of familiarity and kinship in this foreign land whose formality turns family into strangers. They consider it a blessing that you would show up because you felt like it, just because, without needing to ask permission. They looked down their noses at people who acted like goras, making appointments to see each other, like they were visiting a doctor rather than a friend. They saw it as putting on airs.

Generosity and graciousness were important qualities of hosting. You offered your guest not just what you had, but the best of what you had to offer. They'd come to your door, at your mercy, you had to treat them well. This is where things got tricky. What if the best of what you had to offer wasn't technically yours? What if it belonged to someone else in your house, like to your child – could you take it without asking and give it away to someone else? Was that an act of generosity or theft?

It was this conundrum precisely that we confronted on my twenty-third birthday. By this time, we – my siblings and I – had cautiously started celebrating birthdays, in a really low-key way, not with presents and parties but by making gestures of appreciation for the person whose birthday it was. This was tenuous and unstable ground; we walked cautiously around the birthday celebrations, on our best behaviour to ensure that birthday privileges wouldn't be revoked. Sometimes, we celebrated a birthday secretly. On one of her birthdays, my brother snuck my sister out to the Hershey Centre to watch ice-skating. Her eyes still light up when she talks about it all these years later.

My twenty-third birthday was the last birthday I would celebrate while still living at home. I'd been accepted to New York University for doctoral studies and was, against my parents' wishes, moving out that fall. My youngest sister was fourteen at the time, and wanted to celebrate. She loved baking cakes and knew of my obsession with cheesecakes, so she baked me one for my birthday. She put a lot of time and energy into the enterprise. She searched and found a recipe – this was the era before Google – asked my dad to buy her the necessary ingredients and baked a cake. She decorated it with red icing, writing 'Happy Birthday Ayesha' on top. Then she covered it delicately with plastic wrap and announced that she was putting it in the fridge to eat after dinner. We were excited, a reward for the end of the day. I was moved by the gesture, touched by this act of kindness and love, which made me feel special. Feeling special feels really good.

It was a beautiful spring day. I love having my birthday in April. It is such a transitional time of year on the East Coast. The ground is beginning to thaw, there are tiny buds on trees, some flowers are already blooming, the smell in the air is of resurrection. We prayed Asr as a family – it's the prayer offered in the afternoon, when a shadow is twice the length of the body. The fact that the sun and shadows play such a crucial role in determining prayer times reminds us that Islam originated in the desert, where you're guaranteed to see your shadow. This is not an East Coast religion, where heavy, low clouds dominate the skies, blotting out the sun for weeks on end.

Just as we finished Asr, the doorbell rang. Visitors. A mother and her two young children, a one-year-old and a four-year-old. This woman was a student of my mother's, she was a recent immigrant from Pakistan. She attended my mother's Sunday morning class, where a group of South Asian women studied the Qur'an, memorising the meaning of each Arabic word in Urdu. The Qur'an, in this class, was like a giant vocabulary list, so that if students learned the Urdu translation of every single Arabic word, then they would be able to understand the Qur'an when they heard it recited. This technique of Arabic language instruction is called 'Tarjuma Qur'an' (Qur'an in translation), and I learned the Qur'an like this from my mother. My mother also offered commentary on each verse under study, based on her own readings, experiences and opinions. Sometimes she'd say, *Mawlana Maududi says this verse means x, but I think he wasn't seeing the full picture* . . .

So, anyways, this young mother came to our house after Asr prayers because she was missing her own mother and wanted to get out of the house. My mother welcomed her warmly and quickly started to boil water and milk – separately – for chai, relishing the pressure of providing hospitality for a guest with what was at hand. We told our mother we were heading upstairs while she socialised with this unexpected guest, but please, could she get rid of her before dinner? We wanted it to be a family dinner. We had to ask, because it was likely that she would invite the woman to stay for as long as she wanted. My mother glowered at us, angry at our lack of generosity and graciousness.

We went upstairs and hung out until we heard the guests leave. Thankfully, she hadn't stayed for dinner, though I am certain my mother invited her to join us, likely more than once. As we began prepping for dinner, my sister went to pull the cake out of the fridge. She wanted it to sit out for a bit so she could serve it at room temperature.

She shrieked, *What happened to my cake, Mommy?!*

My mother was nonchalant. *What? Oh, I gave a piece to the kid. He wanted some.*

My sister was beside herself. She was crying, upset that her hard work had been ruined. She'd had a vision of how this evening would go, how she'd feel when she served the cake. And now, instead of looking like it had been baked for me for my birthday, it looked like some leftover cake that had already been picked through. And all this because some random person decided to show up to our house, unannounced, and my mother offered her the best of what she had, even though the best of what she had wasn't really hers to offer.

You didn't have to give him the cake! my sister cried. *You could have given him anything else. He didn't even know about the cake! It was a birthday cake!*

My mother yelled back, the mood in the house turning angry and sour. Storm clouds gathered in her face. *Who cares about birthday cakes? So what if there is a piece missing from it? Why are you so stingy? I didn't raise you to be this way!*

It can't have a piece missing from it because it is a birthday cake! You ruined my cake!

Why can't it have a piece missing? Who came up with that rule? This is why we don't celebrate birthdays, we're not goras! What's there to celebrate anyways? You're a year closer to death. You should be crying rather than celebrating. What have you to show for all your years?!

I sat at the kitchen table, hot tears rolling down my face as I looked at the cheesecake in its rectangular Pyrex dish, a corner piece missing.

This is how I'll always remember my twenty-third birthday, I thought melodramatically. *Why can't anything be easy? Why does everything have be a big deal? Why can't we just celebrate a fucking birthday without drama?!*

We had a sober dinner and ate the cake quietly. Later, we laughed about the incident, but not without pain. Before long, our entire family would celebrate Sibghatullah's fourth birthday in Las Vegas. We celebrated the night before, because for some reason I was getting married on his birthday. There were party hats for the four kids running around, there was delicious food and my sister's two-bedroom apartment felt full to the brim with fifteen people talking, laughing and eating. Rumee and I bought Sibghatullah a small boom box as a present, and Rumee showed him how he could carry it on his right shoulder and walk around with it, looking cool. Sibghatullah was shy, smiling sweetly as he tried to carry the boom box on his shoulder, which looked enormous on his tiny frame. His attempt to imitate Rumee made us all laugh.

Six months later, death would visit our family. Unexpected and unannounced. And we'd stop saying that birthdays meant you were a year closer to death.

I am standing in a room in Credit Valley Hospital. It is late afternoon, the light is turning from blinding brightness to a soft gold. It is filtering through the blinds on to the floor, hitting the hospital furniture – the plastic chairs, the bed covered with thin cotton sheets, the machines and their wires and tubes. There are several older women in the room, some wearing shalwar kameez and chadors, some with burqas. They are crying softly, burying their faces into their chadors and hijabs. A young woman sits on the hospital bed holding a tiny baby. I can't see his face, but I can hear him. There is a sound coming from him that fills the room. It is the sound of laboured breathing. It is the sound of breath being painfully forced out of a tiny body. The sound is so strange, it is barely recognisable as human. I've never heard anything like it and I don't hear it again until decades later, while on a fellowship at Radcliffe. A friend, who is a composer, shares music she's written for a hundred-year-old broken accordion she named Annette. Hearing Annette, I recognise the sound. I have a place for this sound in my head. It is the sound of a child laboriously breathing through failing lungs. It is the sound of a child dying, trying to catch one more breath before he will not breathe again. Others in the room do not hear Annette this way. How could they? They weren't there, in that hospital room with me.

Why am I in this room? I've been brought here by my mother to console the grieving family, to lend another body to carry the grief that is hovering, both already here and about to descend upon this family, to help out in any way that I can. But I'm not needed here. I stand silently and helplessly in the corner. I watch the women look at my mother with trusting eyes. They are grateful she is here. She takes her place next to the young woman holding her dying child. She strokes her arm, recites from the Qur'an, whispers reassuring words to her. Words about the afterlife, words about patience, and fortitude, and faith. The women lean in, they listen, intent, hungry. My mother recites prayers, she offers them vessels to carry their grief, she gives them words that catch and hold their pain in different shapes and sizes and colours.

Hours pass like this. The slow, laborious breath getting slower. Eventually it will stop. It is so clear. So inevitable.

It is only a matter of time. A few hours later, I go home. I get a ride from an aunty, one of my mother's friends. My mother stays. She belongs there, in that room. This is her place. She is needed here. She is providing real comfort and solace.

We have dinner without her at home, pray Isha and go to sleep. She stays there, at the hospital, with the mother and child till 1:00A.M., till after the baby passes, till the body is collected and stored in a refrigerator. Later, the baby's body will be bathed – my mother will do that with some of the other women – and then the men will bury him. When I leave, my mother stays.

She is with her family.

She loves them. She is loved by them. I know that when she passes, there will be others to help me carry my grief. And I will be grateful for her service.

Early Talker

I have always been a talker and I have always gotten in trouble for it. My talking caused me a great deal of anxiety growing up. I'd talk so much that, inevitably, I was bound to say the wrong thing, divulge private information, betray a confidence, say something offensive. Then I'd get in trouble. And yet, try as I might to shut up, I could not. The words just poured out of my mouth in a stream, flowing ceaselessly, spilling everywhere, surrounding me in a pool that threatened to drown.

My family's primary form of entertainment – because we didn't watch TV, play sports, read novels – was socialising. We'd get dressed up to go to one of my parents' friends' homes and we'd spend several hours there, in small apartments in musty buildings perfumed with the fragrance of cumin, sitting on floral-patterned couches, the men smoking and talking politics, raising their voices sometimes in passionate disagreement that sounded like anger to us – that probably was anger, too – the women cooking, serving food (which the men took first), then cleaning the piles of dirty dishes while making chai and serving dessert. These apartments had concrete balconies, and the kids would hang out there, or in one of the kids' bedrooms. If the friends had houses, the men would usually be upstairs, the women and babies on the main floor and the children running around in an unfurnished basement. The complete segregation of men to the top floor made it easier for the women to prepare the food and clean up without worrying about modesty, without worrying about their dupattas slipping off, exposing their heads, or necks, or the shapes of their breasts to the eyes of men.

My problem was that I liked talking more than playing with the kids. I found the kids boring. They would play video games, or with dolls, and that was fine for a bit. But I didn't really get it. My parents weren't into toys. Another fact of economic constraint dressed up as virtue, I suppose. Dolls seemed theologically problematic to them; they were a kind of graven image, as were all images of humans and animals. For a few years, they even refused to take photos. If photos, like statues and drawings of people, encroached upon God's creative skills – only *He* could create humans, we weren't supposed to compete – then dolls posed a pretty serious problem. So, instead of staying in my niche social group at these parties, I'd run to the adults, men and women, and charm them with stories, try to impress them with my Qur'an recitation skills. And sometimes, I'd share information my parents would have preferred to keep private.

You talk too much was a common criticism I got. Sometimes my parents would try to use their words lovingly, patiently, to help me understand that I shouldn't talk so much. They'd warn me before the party, *Now, remember Ayesha, don't talk too much!* Other times, they'd yell at me afterwards. Sometimes, they tried hitting. I think we call that 'spanking'. That's a word invented to make parents feel better about hitting their children. It's funny, the words we conjure up to make violence sound like something else, like virtue, or kindness, or something good.

It was all futile because, even though I desperately wanted to, I could not stop talking. I'd know I was talking too much even as I was doing it. And then I'd get stressed out and talk more. And as we prepared to leave, when everyone was in the foyer, surrounded by a sea of shoes, everybody wiggling their feet into their own pair, bending down, tying laces and clasps, the hosts standing around, hovering, all of us saying our goodbyes, I'd seize the opportunity to secure a verbal agreement from my parents in front of everyone that I hadn't spoken too much and that, at any rate, there wouldn't be any punishment.

I didn't talk too much, did I? I'd ask anxiously and loudly, *I'm not going to get into trouble, right?*

I believed that if I got my parents to agree in front of other adult witnesses, then I'd be spared. My parents laughed uneasily at the questions, half amused, half embarrassed. Later, they made it clear: asking those questions *was* talking too much.

My parents weren't the only ones who thought I talked too much. Others did too. And, as it turns out, they felt comfortable policing my behaviour. In every patriarchal society

– so, in most societies – there is an ideal form of femininity and masculinity, mythical standards that everyone is held to. You'd better belong to one of two genders, male or female. And then you have to act your part. If you don't, people try to set you straight – your peers, your family, perfect strangers. People freak the fuck out when you don't act 'appropriately'. They have fancy words to describe the behaviour of people who don't conform – *uncouth, uncivil, disruptive, dangerous, emotional, uncivilised, irrational, inappropriate, wayward, nashiza, bay haya, undisciplined.*

One of the assignments I offer my students is to invite them to pay attention to the ways they perform their gender in their everyday lives, and once they can see their performance, we wonder what would happen if they 'break' one of these performances. They can break their performance in ways big or small; the point is to observe the interplay between their own performance of gender and the social policing of their behaviour. The exercise, which I did not come up with, is meant to draw attention to how much we police our own behaviour in order to avoid having our behaviour policed by others. My students return to class stunned. Female students are told by their mothers to *sit like a lady* when they place their elbows on the table, or they are asked by their brothers, *Why are you sitting like a dude?* when they sit comfortably on the couch, legs spread apart, arms draped over the back of the seat. Male students are told by four-year-old children, *But you're not a girl*, when they offer to paint nails with them.

In my case, it was an amalgamation of 'Canadian', 'Pakistani' and 'conservative Muslim' values, a particular layered manifestation of overlapping patriarchies, that saw my speaking too much as a problem. One friend of my mother's, Zahida, another Pakistani immigrant who lived in the same building as ours, a building dubbed 'Paki Palace', had a big problem with my chatter. She found it irritating and unbecoming. She hated that I monopolised the conversation when she visited my mother. It bothered her that when she visited, tiny little me would instruct my mother to go ahead and prepare chai for the guest while I entertained her with my Qur'an recitation.

A brief interlude on Qur'an recitation here: essentially, this was me serenading my guests in the only way I knew how. By the time I was born, my parents were following a puritanical version of Islam. They were anti-music as part of their anti-assimilation project. Music was the devil's gateway, his entry point. It made you want to move your body, it made you forgetful of God. It's easy for dancing, which is pleasuring in your body, to slip into sexual pleasure. According to the puritans, there is a straight line from music to sex. Muslims aren't the only ones with this precious insight into the evils of music. And, of course, most Muslims have no problem with music, but I didn't know that. As far as I was concerned, music and Islam were mutually exclusive. So, I grew up with the Qur'an as my music. To this day, I relate to it like that. Whenever I listen to it, which is more and more often as I get older, I am nostalgic and I recite along with gusto and passion and wistful sadness.

At any rate, when Zahida visited, she didn't see me as a child starving for attention, a child with two older siblings and a brother just one and a half years younger than her, a child who at a tender age had to make emotional, physical and psychological room for another, more fragile sibling, after already being the third child herself. No, she saw a spoiled brat whose parents were not disciplining her enough. She saw a child that needed to be 'straightened', 'fixed', for her own good. After all, what an undesirable, ugly quality for a girl to have, the quality of talking too much, of not knowing when to shut the fuck up. So, she decided to take matters into her own hands. If my mother wasn't going to set me straight, Zahida would take on this task for her.

The first step in teaching me a lesson was to find a way for us to be alone, without my mother around. This was going to be difficult. As a rule, my mother was extremely suspicious of other adults around her children. However she came to be this way, she never says. But she did teach us to never trust people. We, her children, absorbed this lesson in our bones. But Zahida nevertheless tried to convince my mother to let me visit her alone; she persisted through all the refusals, pretended to adore me, said that she wanted to spend quality time with me, until, finally, she prevailed. She played the infertility and lonely immigrant cards.

My husband and I are trying to have children, but it's not working. I'm so sad and lonely in this country, please let Ayesha come and spend an afternoon with me, it'll cheer me up.

Cheer me up – دل خوش ہو جائے گا The Urdu expression for this translates literally to *my heart will become happy*.

Won't you please let her come? She'll have so much fun. I'd love to hear her chatter all afternoon.

My mother finally relented. The afternoon I was to go over to Zahida's house, my mother prepped me. I was showered, doused with what turns out to be cancer-causing baby powder, dolled up in a dress. My mother psyched me up for the trip.

You'll have fun at Zahida Aunty's house. She loves kids. You're lucky you get to go over there. Don't worry, I'll be right here and I'll come get you in a few hours. Remember, though, behave like a good girl while you're there. Don't talk too much!

Zahida took me up to her apartment and told me that I had a problem.

You talk too much, she said, *and now you're going to learn a lesson.* She took me to her bedroom closet, where there was a stuffed lobster hanging on a plaque. Her husband had bought it for her when he was on some trip, and she hated it. It creeped her out, so she'd hung it in their closet for some reason.

Now, she took me to the closet, pointed at the lobster and said that it was a monster that would eat me because I talked too much. Then she pushed my struggling body into the closet and locked me in. I was alone in there, in the pitch dark, with an image of the fucking lobster seared in my brain, screaming and crying until I could no longer breathe. The panic filled my chest and my brain, it clouded my vision, so the room became darker still. I kicked and pushed against the door to no end. I don't know how long I was in there. It doesn't really matter, does it? Because children cannot tell time – an hour and a day can feel the same. It felt like eternity. And I wonder now, if I might have passed out from the sheer panic, because I don't remember being freed from the closet. There is no record in my mind of the door opening, light flooding in, of her pulling me out.

I just remember my throat being sore, my voice so hoarse I couldn't speak. She gave me ice-cream and told me I'd better not tell anyone what had happened. If I did, the monster in the closet would know and it would come eat me. I believed her; of course I did. I remember eating that ice-cream. Taking pleasure in its sweetness. It was quiet in my head. I had nothing to say. I walked around her living room, eating that ice-cream, not at all hating or angry or afraid of the woman who had essentially kidnapped and tortured me.

At some point my mother called to check in and asked to speak with me. She says that the minute she heard my voice, she knew that something was wrong. She insisted on coming and getting me right way. When she picked me up, I was subdued, quiet. I wasn't talking. This wasn't like me.

Did you have a good time? she asked. I nodded, yes.

She narrowed her eyes at Zahida. *Did something happen? Is everything alright? Why is she so quiet?*

She's fine, we had a great time. She must be tired.

My mother took me home. I was quiet all evening. I fell asleep and woke up screaming, hysterical, burning up with a fever.

It's going to eat me, it's going to eat me!! I yelled.

What's going to eat you? my parents asked, bewildered. I kept pointing to something in the distance. My parents finally called Zahida in the middle of the night, waking her and her husband.

What did you do to our daughter? She's feverish and saying she's afraid something is going to eat her and she won't tell us what.

Well . . . and she confessed. My parents were furious. They told her to never come around again. They shamed her – rightfully – for traumatising their daughter. They assured me that the stuffed lobster was not a monster and that it could not eat me.

For years after, I recoiled at the sight of lobsters. And my body reacts terribly to strong emotions, often passing out almost before I can register them.

A few years ago, Zahida called my mother. She was visiting Canada from the Emirates, where she had relocated. She has grown daughters now. My mother was polite but firm

– she wasn't interested in making time to see her. There are some things you don't come back from, I guess.

Recently, after I fainted at a reception held by the Dean of the Radcliffe Institute for Advanced Study, my mother wondered out loud if what Zahida did still had a lingering effect on how I handled my emotions. She worries and feels guilty, I suppose, for not protecting me from her psycho neighbour friend. It's not her fault. Though she, too, would have preferred it if I didn't talk so much.

But after all that, after all the scolding, the shaming, the hitting, the traumatising; none of it worked.

I still talk a lot, too much according to some. Just this week, I was in a conversation with Rumee and a senior colleague, a white man, a scholar of Jewish studies. We were discussing the ways in which speech is regulated in formal settings to reduce the free exchange of ideas, and he asked Rumee, *Wouldn't it be great for your relationship if her speech was regulated?* And then he laughed hysterically, as if he'd said something witty.

What's the joke? I wanted to ask.

But I didn't. I stayed quiet.

When I was writing my first book, I spent years reading texts by medieval Muslim male scholars, the respected luminaries of my religious tradition, justifying the right of husbands to hit their wives. Their words cast shadows across my heart.

These luminaries found women threatening. They wanted to snuff out our light, straighten us. They said husbands could hit their wives in order to set them straight, to discipline them. They could hit their wives for 'disobedience'. They could hit them for their 'nushuz', for their 'audacity' and, you guessed it, they could hit them for their 'sharp tongues'.

But they also conceded that husbands would never fully straighten their wives. *Eve was created from the rib of Adam*, these Muslim men said, relying on the Judeo-Christian creation story and ignoring the more egalitarian Islamic one. *And so they are crooked*, they said, *like a rib. Don't try to straighten them too much, lest you break them.*

But try anyway, they said.

I wish I could end by saying that I'm done feeling guilty about talking too much. That, *Damn it, I talk too much and the world is better off for it!* That I celebrate this part of myself, that I thrill in the exhilaration of breaking the moulds of ideal femininities. But the fact of the matter is that traumatic experiences of community policing do real damage. They rob a part of you. They break something inside of you, so that, even after years of therapy and trying to glue those parts back together again, like Humpty Dumpty, it doesn't quite work. The cracks and fractures remain, weak points in your psyche, always susceptible to manipulation, to breaking again.

I'm smarter about talking now. But I often worry about talking too much. A part of me still believes I talk too much. In social settings, I regularly check in with myself to see if I've talked too much, pausing to self-examine. And I watch the men and white people do most of the talking. When I speak – especially if I express an opinion – they look at me, suddenly aware of my presence, like they are seeing me for the first time; they might smile or purse their lips as they say, *You are just too much!* Which, of course, is another way of saying, not enough.

Education

The year I was born, my family joined a cult. And this cult's ideology formed the curriculum of my childhood. The cult's ideology aimed for a political order in which God, not humans, had sovereignty. This utopia was called a 'khilafa', and it was meant be ruled by a man called the 'khalifa'. The cult's ultimate goal was to establish shari'a as a global law, to be followed by everyone on Earth. This dream of the future was fuelled by a dream of the past: before colonialism, dreamed the cult leader, Muslims had been God's vicegerents on Earth. This was the original purpose of human creation; Adam was God's first vicegerent on Earth, and we were meant to continue his legacy through the establishment of the khilafa. But Adam, the original khalifa, never headed up a political organisation or a country, so the idea of the khalifa was only loosely styled on him. The cult viewed khilafa as a promise for justice; in the khilafa, God's law would reign supreme, and since God was just, His law was the only just law.

This might sound scary to some, what with Islamophobia and its concerns about 'creeping shari'a'. But don't worry, the cult's ideology was not inherently violent. In fact, the cult believed in 'neither the ballot nor the bullet' as the ideal course for political action. They wanted a non-violent revolution of the mind that would lead to a political revolution.

You might be wondering too about the use of the word 'vicegerent'. The cult leader insisted on the word 'vicegerent' because his vision of an Islamic state, of the khilafa, was formed in the wake of colonialism. The Queen of England always had someone to represent her and her interests in India, and this person was known as her vicegerent. So, the cult leader, living in India and then later Pakistan, imagined an Islamic State that mimicked the British Empire. He maintained the dream of an empire that dominated the globe, on which the sun never set; he wanted to keep the structures of the British Empire in place, but replace all the key players with Muslims. Muslim supremacy replacing white supremacy. In the khilafa, God took the place of the Queen and the cult leader claimed the role of the khalifa, God's vicegerent, for himself. The cult's 'Islamic' theology was very much forged in the fires of British colonialism. Among the crimes of colonialism is that it stole our imaginations, so that even our imagination of ourselves, even our resistance is fashioned in its image.

The cult was post-colonial, nationalist and Pakistani, adhering to and propagating a puritanical version of Islam. It was a fundamentalist organisation. The cult leader used that word.

We are fundamentalists and proud of it, he said. *We aim to return to the fundamentals of Islam.*

He dreamed, out loud, of a pure, clean, simple Islam. An Islam before modernity, before colonialism, before the confusions of the medieval period, the irregularities of empire and cosmopolitan urban centres, an Islam as pure as its birth, in the desert, to a prophet with a small community. A free and liberating Islam. An Islam as desert spring – clear, cool, refreshing, nourishing.

To join this cult, my parents took a bay'a, an oath of allegiance, to *listen and obey* the cult leader in all matters and to tithe their wealth to him. My dad put his hand in the cult leader's hand, like the men of Medina had put their hands in the Prophet's. They made a promise solidified by physical contact. My mother couldn't put her hand in his, though; cross-gender touching could be nothing but sexual. So, for the women, the cult leader again imitated – poorly – the Prophet. In Medina, Muhammad held a rope to connect himself to the women, playing on the rich imagery of the Qur'an:

وأعتصموا بحبل الله جميعا

Hold fast to the rope of God, all together.

The cult leader couldn't find himself a rope, which was surely more readily available than in the Prophet's time, so instead, he held on to a twisted bed sheet simulating a rope. The bed sheet imitated a rope, and the cult leader imitated the Prophet. He held one end of the sheet as the women held the other. Not touching each other physically, but touching metaphorically, through a sheet impersonating a rope, connected to a man impersonating a prophet. The words they uttered, in a call and repeat fashion, were taken from the Qur'an, the very words the women in Muhammad's own community uttered when they gave the Prophet their allegiance. The words the men said for their oath aren't recorded in the Qur'an, but the women's words are:

> *O Prophet, when the believing women come to you pledging that they will not associate anyone with Allah, and will not steal, and will not engage in illicit sex, and will not kill their children, and will not bring slander concocted between their hands and their feet, and will not disobey you in what is good, accept their pledge and ask forgiveness for them from Allah. Indeed, Allah is Forgiving and Merciful.*

And so, in the living room of an apartment in Toronto, South Asian men and women play-acted, repeating the words and the roles of the Prophet and his early community, a prophet whose religion would grow wildly, flourishing for almost 1,500 years now, becoming one of the world's largest religions. Now, some adherents of this religion, a few of over a billion, sat on the floor, trying to recreate the feelings of that first community. They felt echoes of the persecution of that community, and they shared the urgent, feverish dream that their future could be changed by a new belief. If these women sitting on the floor, draped in chadors and hunched over in humbled and submissive postures, gripping the twisted sheet and repeating the words of the Oath of Allegiance, were like the Arabian women who took the Oath of Allegiance recorded in the Qur'an over 1,400 years ago, then maybe the heavyset man who sat on a chair, tall, looking down at the women, and uttering the words they were to repeat, maybe he was like the Prophet. Not *the* Prophet, of course, but surely he fancied himself, at least, *a* prophet.

Uff. I'm struggling to tell this story of my family and the cult. I need to tell it because it is part of my story, it explains so much of who I am, but I resent telling this story because it is too perfect. It gets too much attention. It is titillating and exciting. Some of my white friends love this story. I've been asked to tell it at dinner parties, and I've used it to sing for my supper, offered it as a course to be consumed. But over the years, I find myself telling the story less and less. Even though this story forms me to my core, I hate that it also fulfils stereotypes of Muslims in our particular political moment. And though this experience is an essential part of my personal story, it is marginal, exceptional among Muslims. It doesn't represent mainstream Islam or Muslims. Cults, by definition, are not mainstream. But in other ways, this is a universal story, a story about belonging and alienation, about finding community and meaning in the construction of a life.

This story gives me strength, but it is also a source of weakness. It gives me credibility, but it also gets me the sort of attention I'd rather not attract. The attention of racist people who do not think of themselves as racist at all, and think of me as too courageous, too brave, for becoming the person I have become. I'm not looking for admiration, I do not care for this kind of attention. I ask you, dear reader, to please avoid simplistic, exotic, dehumanised conclusions from this story. Try to find yourself in it. Look harder. You are here.

Okay, back to the story. After a decade of trying to assimilate into Canada, the year I was born, my parents finally gave up. They traded in their racial identifiers for religious ones. It's not that they gave up on being brown – how could they? – but they gave white Canada something else to identify them with. Rather than just being 'Pakis', they became 'Muslims'. Now, when people saw them, they'd notice their attire – strange, foreign, Muslim. My dad's long beard and my mother's hijab.

This was a power move. They inverted the assimilation game and, in doing so, they tried to invert the hierarchy, so that instead of being underneath, looking up at the racists who rejected them, they were above, peering down at Canadians who lived their lives without the truth and enlightenment of Islam. Every time racist white people hurled insults at them, technically, my parents had something to feel good about. They were facing hatred because of something they were choosing to do. And it was worth something, this religious persecution – it accrued them religious merit points. Every racist, hateful, bigoted encounter deposited piety points to their religious bank accounts. And Muslims who successfully assimilated into white Canadian culture became failures; they were weak, lost people who had too readily given up the sacred and precious treasure of Islam in the pursuit of false idols.

But the irony is that the religious identity my parents fashioned in resistance to racism was formed by that racism. It was a new religious identity, an identity encountered, learned and embraced in Canada; not one they had been raised with in Pakistan. In their attempt to outmanoeuvre white supremacy, they submitted to it, moulded themselves to it, created an entirely new identity for it. They became, in some ways, the very caricatures of 'Muslim' conjured up by white people – in their literature, their movies, their popular imagination.

My parents' decision to change their strategy from assimilation to anti-assimilation can be traced back to a particular moment, to a Jumu'a prayer at the Jami' Mosque in downtown Toronto. My father wasn't a very religious man. He did not pray five times a day. But somehow, one Friday afternoon, he found himself at the masjid for Jumu'a. The man delivering the khutba that day happened to be a Pakistani medical doctor turned religious scholar. He had no formal degrees in Islamic Studies. It turns out there are a good number of medical doctors who fancy themselves religious authorities. I guess they figure, *I'm smart, my perspective is probably better than that of the average person.* And they're used to

playing God in their profession, used to receiving the suppli-
cation and gratitude of their patients and their families. But
they should know better – just like having a body doesn't
make you a medical expert, being religious doesn't make you
a scholar of theology.

On the Friday my father decided to go to Jumu'a, the
man delivering the khutba was just such a medical expert.
He was a doctor by the name of Israr Ahmed and he believed
that his perspective and experience made him a religious
authority, worthy of reverence and obedience. Before the
creation of Pakistan, Israr Ahmed had been a member of a
fundamentalist political party in India with the highly uncrea-
tive name Jamaat-e-Islami (The Islamic Group). Soon after
1947, Jamaat-e-Islami's leader, Maulana Maududi, made a
controversial decision to run his party in the upcoming
Pakistani elections. Israr Ahmed viewed Maududi's decision
to participate in the electoral process as a betrayal. If the end
goal was khilafa, with the intention of returning sovereignty
to God, then participating in a democratic political process
that ceded sovereignty to human beings betrayed the cause.
Instead, he argued, a khilafa must be run by a khalifa, someone chosen not by a vote, but by the strength of his religious
convictions. After all, the khalifa was supposed to represent
God, not the people. According to him, voting for the khalifa, making him accountable to people's whims, made a
mockery of the whole system.

Branding Maududi a moderate sell-out, Israr Ahmed
created his own political religious group. Carrying on the

unimaginative tradition of fundamentalism everywhere, he named this new group Tanzeem-e-Islami (The Islamic Organisation). Tanzeem, he said, would never sell out its core message that sovereignty belongs only to God. They would work tirelessly to bring about a revolution that would establish a khilafa that would truly represent God on Earth. And as the leader and mastermind of the movement that would establish this khilafa, it stood to reason that Israr Ahmed himself would be the ideal khalifa.

Israr Ahmed's message caught on among enough people that he started forming local chapters of his Tanzeem in various cities, first in Pakistan, and then increasingly abroad. Some chapters had five or six members, whereas others had hundreds. In 1979, he was visiting some of his acolytes in the Toronto chapter, and happened to be delivering the khutba the day my dad decided, on a whim, to show up to a masjid in downtown Toronto for Jumu'a. A masjid that had itself converted, not long before, from a church to a mosque.

Israr Ahmed was a fiery, charismatic preacher. He was a rotund man, and he stuck his tummy out when he stood, arching his back like he was pregnant. He had a deep bari-tone voice, almond-shaped eyes and dark brown skin. He sported a beard that was beginning to whiten and a Qaid-e-Azam hat, which is sort of like the cap naval officers wear but made of lambswool. Israr Ahmed preached a version of Islam that was anti-colonial, Pakistani nationalist and Salafi. He saw a return to the fundamentals of Islam as the solution to all problems – not just the problems of Muslim communities, but of all humanity. A simple, clear, universal solution to all problems, past and future. And Muslims, especially Pakistanis, had a special role to play in this solution. According to Israr Ahmed, God created Pakistan as a homeland for Muslims, and its destiny was to be the seat of the khilafa that would bring peace and justice to the world. But for that dream to be realised, we first needed to stop being ashamed of our Islam and of being Pakistani.

Don't dilute and change your ways, be strong, be proud of yourselves, he told the congregants. *Why would you try to be like white people and Christians and secularists? You're not lost, they are! You shouldn't be following them, they should be following you!*

My father connected deeply with this message. This was the belonging he'd been searching for the whole time, except that he'd had it upside down. Instead of trying to assimilate, he should have been trying to resist assimilation. He was special. He was important. He had a crucial, even historic role to play. He was Muslim. He was Pakistani. He had the cure for what ailed humanity right at his fingertips. He could become a leader, the one who got respect, the one whom others followed. Israr Ahmed would show him the way. But first he'd need to join his Tanzeem, take an oath of allegiance, promise to *listen and obey*, tithe his wealth and join a local chapter, called an 'usra', which means 'family'.

My father is an easily excitable man. It's one of the things that makes him both lovable and exasperating. When he felt his heart soar at the message of Israr Ahmed, like a helium balloon floating into the sky, he didn't stay on the ground, looking up, watching it float away. Nope. He jumped up and caught the string and floated with it, into the unknown, wherever it might take him. After the khutba, a group of men spontaneously pledged their allegiance to Dr Israr Ahmed. My father was one of them.

That evening, he hurried home to tell my mother about Israr Ahmed, and Tanzeem-e-Islami, his new family, and our new life path.

My mother was always the more religious of my parents. She'd been pulled out of eighth grade to become a full-time caregiver for her maternal grandfather. He was blind and needed full-time care. At first, my khala, my mother's sister, cared for him. But then she got married off and it was decided that my mother would be his caregiver. It goes without saying that this decision was made for her, she was not consulted. She didn't want to be pulled out of school. She loved school. Her father made the decision. She says that when she heard the news, she cried for days. He waited her out. Eventually, she ran out of tears and realised that her resistance was futile. Her father's mind was made up and there was no way around it. She eventually got over her grief and went upstairs to her grandfather's room, ready to care for him. He apologised to her, said he knew she was sad and that he'd rather that she not have to sacrifice her education for him.

But she did. And he let her.

Patriarchy is cruel to women in such complex ways. In a patriarchal culture, women's education is of little value. If you're just going to be married off to produce children, then education is a luxury that can easily turn into a burden. Education requires investment of the family's resources – money, time, labour – for little return. Girls' time can be better spent learning practical skills. Instead of sitting in a classroom and poring over homework, they could be learning to cook and mend clothes. The monetary investment in school fees and uniforms, notebooks, pens, etc., have little value if you aren't expected to enter the workforce and provide for the family. So you can see how this trade-off between education and free labour made for an easy choice for my grandfather. I doubt he agonised over his decision.

But the only reason he was faced with this choice to begin with was because of a failure of patriarchy. You see, my mother's blind maternal grandfather, my great-grandfather, was the responsibility of his son, not his daughter. And my great-grandfather had a son who was a wealthy businessman who had the means to care for him, and in fact offered to do so. But this son wanted to hire help to provide that care, and my great-grandfather found this insulting. He was disappointed and ashamed that his very own son, whom he had *raised with his own hands*, with an over-abundance of love and care, would abandon him in his old age to the care of hired help. He wanted not only to live in his son's house, but to be looked after by his son – which really meant, cared for by his son's wife and daughters.

This is a theme that finds itself in the nursing-home debate currently raging in South Asian immigrant communities. The expectation is that in old age, people receive fundamentally different care from their relatives than they do from strangers. Strangers, also known as 'professionals', don't love the people they are caring for, they are not indebted to them, they cannot be readily manipulated by guilt and shame. Of course, this is not a self-evident truth – that you receive better care from loved ones than from paid professionals. And elder abuse by family members and professionals alike is a real phenomenon. But the conceit that family takes better care of you is strong, rooted in a mythical conception of the 'family' as a womb-like place, a simple place of symbiotic love and respect. Where parents are gods who only want what is best for their children, who sacrifice everything for them, and who are then rewarded, in the end, with obedient children whose happiness springs from caring for and serving their parents. To hire help, or to – god forbid – put one's parents in a nursing home, ruptures the myth of the family and is thus a vile, unforgivable sin. Human weaknesses, and desires, and constraints, and failings, and limitations have no place in the myth of the family.

It was this myth laid bare, exposed as false, that was at play in the conflict between my blind great-grandfather and his son, that landed my great-grandfather at his daughter Rehmat's doorstep. He arrived in the afternoon, unguided, by himself, vulnerable and alone, dignity in hand, at the mercy of his daughter's fiery-tempered husband, Asad-ur-Rehman.

Only Rehmat was home when he arrived. He said:

رحمت کمرہ چاہیے، کمرہ دے سکتی ہو؟ *, Rehmat, I need a room, can you spare a room?*

Rehmat said, کمرہ ہے، لیکن پوچھنا پڑے گا *There is a room, but I'll have to ask first.*

Disappointed by her answer, my great-grandfather headed out, but as he was leaving, he ran into Asad-ur-Rehman, who was just returning home. Asad-ur-Rehman took his father-in-law's hand and asked, *What's going on? Have you had chai?*

No. I came to ask Rehmat for something.

Well, come back in, have some chai!

Over chai, Asad-ur-Rehman asked, *So, what did you come to ask for?*

I came to ask for a room.

What did she say?

She said she had to ask you first.

My grandfather took his father-in-law's hand a second time that afternoon and walked him around the house, telling him the measurements of each room, the number of windows, telling him, *Any room you want in this house is yours.*

Asad-ur-Rehman was annoyed with his wife, that she hadn't just said *yes* to her father, that she didn't know that her husband was the kind of magnanimous and generous man who would of course accommodate his father-in-law's request.

But she didn't know. So she had to ask.

In addition to a room, Asad-ur-Rehman also offered up his daughter, my khala, to be his father-in-law's primary caregiver. After a few years, my khala was arranged to be married. As she sat in the courtyard, on a takht-posh, at her rukhsati – which is a sort of 'send-off', where the girl leaves her family to now live with her husband and his family – Asad-ur-Rehman found himself overcome with emotions, and his eyes welled up. As he wiped away his tears, he noticed his blind father-in-law crying too. He was confused.

I'm crying because my daughter is leaving, تسی کیوں روے ہو؟ *Why are you crying?*

His father-in-law replied, آج میں محتاج ہو گیا *Today I've become dependent, a burden,* because his primary caregiver was leaving the house, being married off.

Without any hesitation, Asad-ur-Rehman offered up his youngest daughter, my mother.

You're not muhtaj, میرے پاس ایک اور بیٹی ہے *I have one more daughter.*

And so, in another act of dramatic generosity, Asad-ur-Rehman screwed my mother out of an education. Even though her grandfather would apologise to her for this unfortunate situation, he effectively made it happen by refusing the care of hired help, by demanding that his full-time caregiver share his blood. A family member had to be sacrificed for his demands.

In some ways, my mother made peace with this traumatic event. She certainly forgave both her father and her grand-father. Indeed, she speaks highly of them, reverentially, even. It meant a lot to her that her father cried when, some years later, he stumbled upon her notebooks and saw her fine penmanship. He said he wished he hadn't pulled her out of school.

And my mother loved those few years with her grandfather. He was a highly organised and well-disciplined man. In her memories, he lived his days in a regimented fashion, was strict about his diet, ate only a small amount at fixed times. If a meal was late, he'd skip it. This behaviour could be seen as childish and vengeful, but she saw it as noble. Since he was blind, he loved being read to, to pass the time. So my mother read to him from weekly magazines, some of which were put out by Jamaat-e-Islami. These magazines were full of the teachings of political Islam, especially those of the founder of Jamaat-e-Islami, Maulana Maududi. The teachings in these magazines formed the foundation of my mother's knowledge about Islam. They taught her how a Muslim should behave and this understanding was deeply gendered, with Muslim women playing supporting roles for their husbands, and fathers, and brothers, and sons. Later, she would struggle with these values as an immigrant trying to assimilate into Canada. And when she finally decided to ditch the assimilation project, these values gave her a soft place to land. Tanzeem offered her a sense of purpose and control, a sense of belonging to something greater than family, a chance to be part of a movement, to become an actor in history, a way to move beyond her domestic role of caregiver.

Despite the warm memories of caring for her grand-father, my mother lamented being pulled out of school for the rest of her life. She tried going back when her first two children started school themselves. I think she imagined a different future for herself, apart from the roles of mother and wife. She enrolled at a local high school, but the language barrier was difficult to overcome. She struggled to fulfil her duties as a mother and wife alongside school. And my dad's brother and a friend, who were living with them at the time, whom my parents had sponsored from Pakistan, who were sharing my parents' tiny apartment and eating their food, mocked her when she'd come home from school. Rather than helping out, they derided her dreams. Who did she think she was, that she'd get a chance to go to school again, get an education? Did she think she could get a job? It all proved too much.

A few years ago, I enrolled her in adult education English classes. I took her to her first class. She was scared, but she is brave. She stuck with the classes for four years, waddling to school with her bad knees, wearing a jilbab and hijab. She finished grade twelve English. But she didn't take the extra few classes necessary to get a high school diploma. She was overwhelmed with fear at having to take a mathematics course; math scared her. It's not the numbers and the equations that scared her so much as the very real possibility that she might not be good at it, or, even worse, work hard at it and still fail. She doesn't want to fail or to be at the start of things. I get it. It's exhausting when so many of life's basic experiences are new and unfamiliar. Easier and safer to stick to what you know and come to terms with how life turned out.

Still, she did well for herself. She put six children through university. She became a religious scholar in her own right. She taught herself Qur'anic exegesis, reading Qur'an commentaries in Urdu, in her basement study, poring over books, transcribing audio lectures verbatim. She's taught Qur'an classes in that basement for several decades, and continues to do so today. She taught generations of children to recite the Qur'an. She's educated dozens of women in her Sunday classes, where they study Qur'an translation and interpretation. And she has lectured on the Qur'an to all-female audiences on the first Saturday of every month for three decades now.

When people ask me how I came to be a professor in Islamic Studies, the answer is obvious. I'm just trying to be like my mother.

I don't know much about my father's past. He was born in India, we don't know what year exactly. He was named after an older brother he never met. His older brother was around eighteen years old and bathing in a talaab (reservoir) on farmlands nearby when he drowned. People said that Hindu and Sikh boys held him under water until he died. My father was his namesake and his stories swirled around my father's childhood.

When he was around five years old, my father's family fled to Pakistan. His father, my paternal grandfather, heard about the coming inter-religious and ethnic violence that accompanied Partition, where mobs burned villages, killed everyone in their path, where butchers and neighbours and friends and teachers slaughtered long-held, respected clients, and neighbours and friends and students. My grandfather started slowly selling his precious household items in preparation for the moment they'd have to flee. When word came that the mobs were close, a group of families fled together, staying in refugee camps along the way, until the violence approached again, and then they hopped trains until, finally, they disembarked together, in a city in Pakistan called Toba Tek Singh. My father went to school until twelfth grade, and then he got a diploma in metallurgical arts. His art: welding.

My father had no dreams of coming to Canada, but found himself filling out an application for a visa when visiting the Canadian embassy with a friend who wanted to move there. *Why not submit an application, too?* his friend asked. So he applied. His friend didn't get a visa, but my father did – Canada needed welders.

When my father went in for the interview, the officer asked him, *Where do you want to go in Canada?*

My father replied with a question, *Where are the jobs?*

Toronto.

I'll go there, then.

So he moved to Toronto. He went back to Pakistan to get married and returned with my mother. He had his children in Toronto. He met Israr Ahmed in Toronto. He found meaning for his life in Toronto. Tanzeem gave my father a purpose, a sense of belonging to something bigger than himself. It made him less lonely. Each local chapter was called an 'usra', a 'family', and the members did what they could to make it feel that way. In diaspora, Tanzeem was a lifeline.

My father spent most of his life at his job, working long, hard hours, toiling with his body, negotiating social terrain from a low rung on the social hierarchy. He spent his free time making copies of Israr Ahmed's audio tapes, selling or distributing them for free to friends and others at various mosques. Israr Ahmed's message was for Muslims, it was meant to convert Muslims first and foremost. My father bought boxes of TDK cassette tapes, each wrapped in shiny black and red packaging. He gingerly opened the covers, he pulled at the little tab that makes for easy removal, he carefully labelled and recorded the tapes. At first, he recorded the cassettes one by one on a tape recorder, but then he bought an expensive and fancy machine that made three copies of each cassette at once, and in a matter of minutes. He spent hours making those tapes. Sometimes we would join him, a family production. Then, at Eid prayers, or Jumu'a, or at Muslim bazaars, we'd distribute them, trying to convince other, weaker, lost, failing Muslims to join us, to join our Tanzeem. Most of them weren't into it, but once in a while we got some new members. It felt like sweet victory. Immediately, we'd treat them like family, because they were in our usra now. Our family. We didn't need to build trust, take time to learn about each other first, because we were already family, we were committed to the same cause. Khilafa. God's sovereignty. Justice on Earth. We had taken an oath on the same man's hand. We would visit each other's houses. My mother would lecture the women, and my father would play Israr Ahmed's cassettes for the men. The women would listen to my mother's lectures, sometimes willingly, other times resentfully, and the men would sit around silently listening to the tapes. Inevitably, there would be fallings out, betrayals, raised voices, hurt feelings.

In time, like Hajra so many centuries ago, we learned that our shared values, expressed in the ritual of communal oath-taking, were not enough to make a family. An oath taken on the hand of the same man does not always prove lasting. Imagined values cannot do the work that blood fails to do. In the end, we would learn, family is elusive and illusory. Like a mirage in the desert that looks like water but is just hot air and our eyes tricking us. And Hajra, abandoned with her son, searching frantically for water, her mouth dry and parched, her heart lonely, and heavy with disappointment.

Ultimatum

Memory is a funny thing. It plays tricks on you, makes you remember things that never happened or forget things that did. But it isn't memory that plays these tricks on us. It's us. We play tricks on ourselves and then blame it on memory. The truth, reality, is so unbearable sometimes that we'd rather believe something else. So we often rewrite our pasts, make up stuff, delete things, believe in our own edits, such that they begin to form us, influence our present and future.

Sometimes, we make up temporary stories to suit our purposes, fortify our psychological well-being for the time being, but then we can lose the narrative. With love and support, we can gain the strength to go back and revisit the past, take a second look, undo the edits and try to accept the past as it happened, rather than how we wish it had gone.

I feel this way about my niqab story. Why did I wear it? How did I feel about wearing it? Was I forced to wear it? Did I want to wear it? The answers to these questions have changed for me over the years.

The niqab is a face veil and our cult leader, Dr Israr Ahmed, said that God intended for women to wear it. In general, my parents thought Israr Ahmed's interpretations of the Qur'an were definitive. If he said it, it must be true. Israr Ahmed's wife and daughters, all of whom lived in Pakistan, wore niqab. They were super pious, the most pious. And their piety reflected on him. *His* wife and *his* daughters wore niqab. What a great man.

My mother didn't want to be outdone by their piety. She's a very competitive person and channels her competitiveness through religious fervour. She wanted to be 'the best' at being a cult member, the model female Muslim. But she lived in Canada, and it was far more difficult to wear niqab in Canada than in Pakistan. No one harassed you for wearing niqab in Pakistan. If you were walking on the street wearing a niqab, no one would call you a 'terrorist', no one would tell you to go back to your country. No one wrote opinion pieces in national newspapers, throwing fits about seeing a niqabi on the subway. No one said that wearing the niqab made you inferior, less than, oppressed, stupid, without agency, a non-person – at least, not to your face. But in Canada, all of these things happened. Even before 9/11, before it became politically expedient to equate Islam with terrorism. Even while we were still basking in the afterglow of the Afghan Freedom Fighters visiting the White House.

My mother asked Israr Ahmed what he thought about Muslim women wearing niqab in Canada, where we would be persecuted for wearing it. He said that if our faith was really strong, we'd wear it anyways. And yes, we'd face persecution, but whatever we faced would be nothing compared to what the Sahaba, the Companions of the Prophet, faced for following Muhammad.

Think of Bilal, he said, *lying in the desert, with a huge boulder placed on his chest.* Bilal, the enslaved Ethiopian, tortured by his enslaver for embracing the light of Islam. He persevered, survived, and the Prophet made him the mu'azzin for the community. He called the believers to prayer. What an honour, what a great reward for enduring torture.

But if it is too hard to wear niqab in Canada, Israr Ahmed offered, *God is forgiving.* He would take this into account. Maybe He'd choose to forgive us if we were too weak, too scared to follow His command.

This put my mother in a difficult position. She had the option of accepting that her faith wasn't strong enough to wear niqab in Canada and hope for God's mercy in the Hereafter, when her deeds were being weighed in the scales. The good deeds on the right side, the bad deeds on the left. Which way would the scales tip, deciding her eternal fate? Would she end up in Heaven or Hell? She could gamble on God's mercy or she could demonstrate the strength of her faith by wearing niqab in Canada, an easy physical marker that proved to the world how great her faith was, and accept, submit to whatever discrimination came her way. And remember that at least she had it better than Bilal. The enslaved black Muslim tortured by his Arab master in the desert in the seventh century. And count her blessings, for they were many. Starting with not being enslaved.

My mother really wanted to wear niqab in Canada. But she didn't want to do it by herself; she wanted her daughters to wear it as well. There is strength in numbers. She often said,

ایک اکیلا، دو گیارہ

One is alone, but two is eleven. It works in Urdu.

So she waited for us to grow older so we could all wear niqab together. A family of niqabis. A family ostracised together. My mother dreamed of having an exemplary, legendary Muslim family that would be remembered through the ages for the strength of their faith. How would people know we had such tremendous faith? By our niqabs, of course. They wouldn't see our faces, but they'd see our faith. We'd be known as a Muslim family, a believing family, a family whose women all wore niqabs, even in Canada, in a land of disbelievers. A family that preserved its piety and purity even while surrounded by temptations. I imagine my mother's vision of our perfect family, niqabi women, niqabi daughters and niqabi granddaughters, riding off into the sunset. And my mother, the great matriarch, leading us all.

I wore niqab for ten years, from tenth grade to the end of my master's. Through public high school and two degrees at a public university. I faced a lot of discrimination for wearing niqab. From my teachers, from peers, from strangers. I had to answer a lot of questions about the niqab, so I needed a clear narrative that responded to the intrusive and persistent queries I fielded, all the time, whether I wanted to or not.

The story of the niqab as told in my family goes like this: my older sister was the one who mustered up the courage to wear niqab to high school. My quiet, shy, but also incredibly strong-willed older sister. I have found that those qualities often go hand in hand. She's the one who decided she didn't want to live a life of *cognitive dissonance*, of *hypocrisy*, of *nifaq*, of believing one thing and doing another. If she believed that God demanded she wear a face veil, well, she would wear it. Come what may. She couldn't square not wearing the niqab for the sake of people who didn't share her values to begin with. Why should she be trying to please them when she meant to please God?

My mother was impressed by her, in awe of her. If her daughter was willing to wear niqab and suffer the conse-quences – derision, mockery, discrimination, abuse – what was stopping her from wearing it, too? So my mother supported my sister's decision and started wearing it herself.

And when I came of age, in tenth grade, I joined my mother and sister willingly. Why wouldn't I? I shared their beliefs. I wanted to follow Islam. And I lived in a free country. When an old white man at a gas station walked over to me, with great effort, his hands trembling, meaning to speak to me, and I leaned in to listen, out of deference for the elderly, and he said, *Do you know you don't have to wear that in this country?* I replied, *Do you know I'm allowed to wear this in this country?*

No, I'm not being forced to wear niqab! I told people when they asked, *Are you being forced to wear that?* – asking the coded question, a question meant to confirm their racist and bigoted beliefs about Muslims, as backward and oppressive and misogynist.

I didn't want to confirm these beliefs because I knew them to be false. So, what else could I say? I only had one answer available to me, so I said, *I* want *to wear niqab. I believe Muslims are supposed to wear it, so that is why I'm wearing it.*

I even came up with a nice, clean backstory for it. I was in ninth grade and at Jumu'a prayers when I happened upon a cute little copy of the Qur'an in translation. It had gold-leaf edging, and having been published in Saudi, it was practically printed on oil. Its pages were thick and shiny. I had to have it, so I bought it. And then I encountered the verse in the Qur'an that, I would later learn was actually quite vague about what women should wear, but was translated in this cute little fundamentalist Qur'an in clear, precise and unambiguous language.

The verse reads:

يـأيها النبى قل لأزواجك وبناتك ونساء المؤمنين يدنين عليهن من جلبيبهن ذالك أدنى أن يعرفن فلا يؤذين ۞

O Prophet! Tell your wives, and daughters, and the believing women, that they should cast their outer garments over themselves: this is better, so that they may be recognised and not harassed / hurt.

But the Saudi translation read:

> *O Prophet! Tell your wives and your daughters and the women
> of the Believers to draw their cloaks (veils) all over their
> bodies (i.e. screen themselves completely except the eyes or one
> eye to see the way). That will be better, that they should be
> known (as free respectable women) so as not to be annoyed.*

As a ninth grader, I wasn't yet tuned into the fact that all
translation is interpretation, or aware of the politics of religious knowledge production, or how authoritarian regimes
rely on patriarchal interpretations of religion to protect
their power; so I just assumed that the translation was the
Qur'an itself, as if it had not been mediated and tampered
with by men. If the Qur'an said that Muslim women should
cover everything except their eyes, and if I was a Muslim
woman, then it followed that I should wear a niqab. So I
wore it. It was as simple as that.

It was hard to wear niqab in Canada, but that was
because of racism, not Islam. If people just left me alone,
stopped being cruel and mean, then I'd be just fine. It
wouldn't be so hard.

My niqab was a mirror of sorts; people couldn't see my
face, but it revealed truths about themselves, like the limits
of their tolerance, their willingness to be open, accepting,
respectful of values different from their own. Most people
recoiled at what they saw in my niqab, but they were only
recoiling at the vision of themselves revealed by it. And then

they either dug in their heels, or tried to be better. In all cases, they used me as a medium to prove their goodness, their well-meaning intentions, even if those intentions were expressed in vile words and ugly actions. It was exhausting. Wearing niqab in Canada was fucking exhausting.

Parts of the story I've just told you are true. But there are parts missing. And then there are parts that are just made up. One thing that is made up is that I encountered this verse in ninth grade – in fact, I was raised with a patriarchal interpretation of this verse. Another made-up fact is that I wanted to wear niqab, that I wasn't pressured into wearing it.

The pressure to wear niqab started for me in middle school. When I was in middle school, I wanted to assimilate into white Canadian culture. I was wearing hijab and trying to get my mother to sew me dresses and long skirts, Anne of Green Gables-style. I wanted to belong, so I figured that if I dressed like white people in the early 1900s, when they still had a modicum of shame and modesty, then maybe people wouldn't notice my hijab first. Maybe they'd just see me as normal, wearing dresses and skirts, i.e. *Western* clothing, even if it was a bit more covering than what my classmates were wearing. I was restricted to skirts and dresses, even in my imagination, because pants were not an option. No matter how loose. Even the suggestion of legs, or my ass, was too sexy to bear.

As my middle school graduation approached, I was excited. I loved the idea of having my name called out, walking alone on to that stage, everyone watching me. That kind of attention was so thrilling to me, it made me ill with excitement. I trembled with anticipation as graduation approached.

In the meantime, my mother and older sister began a campaign to get me to wear niqab once I started high school. I was upset by this. I did not want to wear niqab, especially when starting high school. Why did I have to wear niqab now that the two of them had started wearing it? I felt persecuted. Doubly so. At school I was too Muslim, even without a niqab. And at home, I wasn't Muslim enough, because I was resisting niqab. My resistance was seen as defective faith, making me the weak link in our family's armour, the one who might be easily pierced, the one who might even invite in the enemy.

The tension between me on one side and my mother and sister on the other mounted throughout eighth grade. I felt like they were ganging up on me. I felt like this was really unfair. I barely had any friends to begin with – who'd be my friend once I wore niqab? I'd be so othered. It was hard enough to wear hijab to school, and the clothes sewed by my mother that always made me feel like an outsider, now I had to wear niqab, too?

The tension came to a head in time for graduation. My mother delivered an ultimatum: wear the niqab to graduation or you cannot go at all. This ultimatum, like all good ultimatums, put me in an impossible position. More than anything, I wanted to attend my graduation, have my moment in the spotlight. But now my mother demanded that I make myself unrecognisable in order to attend. Literally unrecognisable – I mean, no one would recognise me, because they wouldn't be able to see my face. They wouldn't know to associate the niqab with me, because I'd never worn it to school. I was hijabi-Ayesha, not niqabi-Ayesha!

This on top of the fact that I'd have to give up on all my outfit fantasies. Whatever the niqab is, well, at least the way my mother sewed it for us anyways, it is a travesty of fashion. I'm South Asian, and like a 'good' South Asian girl, I love my bling. I had spent countless hours fantasising about what I'd wear to graduation: my sparkling shoes, bangles, lacy dress, the long necklaces that I'd wear over my hijab, how I'd tie my hijab – fashionably, of course! And now it was all ruined. If I wore niqab, none of it would matter. I wouldn't get to be myself at my own graduation.

I was filled with deep angst, angst appropriate to a thirteen-year-old child for whom her eighth-grade graduation meant everything, too much – a thirteen-year-old with little perspective. I cried, I pouted. I was mean and unkind, I had a bad attitude. I tried to be pleasing and win my mother over with sweetness and obedience. I tried to play it cool, like I didn't care about my graduation. I grovelled. None of it worked.

I hoped, desperately, that the ultimatum was a bluff.

That my mother would relent and let me go to graduation without niqab. That she wouldn't follow through with her threat. I fabricated hope.

My mother's love and compassion for me were pitted against her ideals and self-image.

This was a big deal for her. She was worried that I wouldn't wear niqab in high school. She believed that if somehow she managed to make me wear it to my graduation, that would be the perfect way to help me transition from hijab to niqab. That's if she was at all thinking about this constructively and worrying about my well-being and about what would be best for me. It's just as likely she was insecure, threatened by my refusal to wear niqab, even once I got to high school. If I didn't wear niqab, how would that reflect on her? Would she be seen as unsuccessful at raising me with the correct values? Also this: my mother was genuinely worried about my well-being in the Hereafter. She wanted to protect me from any possible punishment for not being a good enough Muslim. She was literally, in her mind, trying to save her daughter's flesh from burning in fire, also known as Hell. Hell is a real thing for those who believe in it. They might do unspeakable things to protect you from it.

My refusal to wear niqab was fucking with her vision of how her family would turn out, the kinds of daughters she had raised and the kind of fate we'd have in the Hereafter.

Or maybe we were just caught in a stubborn to-the-death stand-off that mothers and daughters sometimes find themselves in. No one knows how they got there or how to get out safely.

In the end, we all lost. Everyone always does when an ultimatum is delivered. I couldn't bring myself to wear niqab to graduation, so I didn't go. I felt terrible. The world felt unfair and cruel. My mother lost too, since she didn't get me to wear niqab. I started ninth grade without it. I don't know how my mother felt about denying me my graduation. Did she struggle with it? Did she feel sorry for me, or did she think I got what I deserved for being so stubborn? Did she feel virtuous for following through with her ultimatum? Did she even think about it?

The pressure to wear niqab from my mother and older sister remained relentless. Maybe my sister was embarrassed that her own sister in high school wasn't covering her face. It was bad enough that the other Muslims at school didn't think that the niqab was necessary, or religiously mandated, or even authentically Islamic. It must have been painful and alienating for her, this misrecognition she experienced from other Muslims. I wonder if what she expected to receive from her Muslim peers was admiration, not judgement and a concerted distancing. And then, on top of that, to have a younger sister in the same high school who didn't wear niqab must have further isolated and alienated her, made her Islam feel marginal.

By tenth grade, I had been worn down. I decided to wear niqab to high school. My mother and sister were proud of me. Thrilled. But I felt defeated, and scared. I really didn't want to deal with the social backlash at school, on the bus, in the streets. But I did. And it made me angry that people couldn't just leave me the fuck alone. That I had to keep talking about, explaining, answering questions about it. My younger sister also started wearing niqab in high school. By the time my youngest sister, the one nine years my junior, started high school, I fought my mother on making her wear niqab, even as I continued to wear it myself in university.

She can wear niqab later, I said, *if she really wants to. But she's too young, in ninth grade, to make that decision.*

Thinking about the kinds of hate she'd encounter was heartbreaking to me. I couldn't bear the thought and thankfully my mother relented. By that time, the influence of the cult on my parents was waning anyway. My mother was getting softer. Age seems to do that to people.

When she hit her sixties, my mother started adult education classes for English. She was nervous about going back to school, but exhilarated at the thought of being in a classroom, meeting people and impressing her teachers. She went for a few years and never once wore niqab to class. As she progressed from one grade level to the next, I listened to her breathless stories about her fellow students and teachers.

The small, petty part of me wanted to yell at her, to

shame her, *Where's your niqab? What happened to your faith? You made us wear niqab, suffer through all those years. Now you can't wear niqab to class even for a day? How dare you?!*

Thankfully, a more compassionate part of me prevailed. I said nothing. I should be happy that she was spared the pain of wearing niqab to her classes. So, I am. Happy, that is.

Scripts

When people ask me why I wore niqab or why I took it off, I rarely tell the truth. People are often not interested in the truth anyways; usually they come to the conversation with ideas they are looking to confirm. Sort of like, *Was it hard to wear it? How hard was it? What's the worst thing that happened? Don't you feel so free now? Thank god you live here, right?*

Or maybe, *So, how was it to take it off? Are your parents disappointed? Do you wish you hadn't taken it off? Do you struggle with shame for removing it?*

Or, as one woman hosting a dinner put it plainly, *Shame on you!*

These conversations, when they are conversations, can feel like a kind of non-consensual dance, where I learn what people want to hear and then try my best not to disappoint them and ruin the evening. I am a reluctant participant because this dance demands I tailor the truth of my experience to a garment that is too constricting. In doing so, I am forced to confront the truth of my experience, a truth that is painful, too difficult even to admit to myself, never mind share with strangers. And too complicated besides.

That first day I put niqab on and looked at myself in the mirror before leaving for school, I saw fear. I was terrified of wearing niqab to school. Terrified of other people's reactions to me, terrified of how they would make me feel. I knew people were going to be mean, and I was afraid of being the object of their cruelty, their fear, their insecurity. It's one of the scariest things I've ever done, wearing niqab in Canada. Every day, securing my niqab before leaving the house was like donning armour before going into battle. Because I could be certain that there would be some confrontation every day – whether it was outright hateful, aggressive, angry behaviour, passive-aggressive shit (I was in Canada, after all) or just well-intentioned, offensive ignorance. The niqab evoked strong reactions in everyone I encountered.

One question I was asked over and over again was whether my parents were forcing me to wear 'that'. Immediately, I knew the correct answer:

No! I choose to wear niqab and my parents are supporting my decision.

I was stuck between stereotypes of Muslim women as backward and oppressed and the misguided ideals of my parents. My mother, influenced by South Asian, post-colonial, Pakistani culture, as well as the Saudi-inflected puritanism of the cult she had joined, believed that the more a woman covered, the more pious, pure and 'Muslim' she and her family were. The more invisible a woman, the better.

The cult leader, Israr Ahmed, told the story, oft-repeated by my mother, of a Pakistani family that was so devout that when the women of the family left their house, they not only wore burqas, so that they were covered from head to toe, but additionally, male servants held up sheets around them as they moved from the gate of their house to the covered carriage that awaited them just outside. The sheets were an added layer of security, meant to protect them from the gaze of strangers passing by. We didn't know anything about these women except for how much they covered, and, in the cult's narrative, that's all we needed to know to measure the devotion and piety of the women and, more importantly, their family.

As with most stories we learn as children, I accepted this one wholesale, without questioning. I admired these women and this family. How pious they must have been! When my mother recounted the tale of these women, her voice brimmed with admiration; she wanted her family to be pious like this family. But for that to happen, we'd need to be as pious as those women, and cover up as much as possible. Her dream and our behaviour were inextricably bound; we could, by our actions or inaction, by what we wore, make or break her dreams. It's never a good situation when others have this much power over our dreams. They are bound to disappoint us. It is inevitable. Still, each time my mother recounted the story of these super pious, invisible, nameless women, we absorbed bits of her dream into our minds, into our bodies.

As I grew older, I started wondering about this story. Who were these women? How many were they? What were their names? Were they good people? Were they kind? What was the quality of their lives? Did they go to school? How, exactly, did the whole sheet thing work when they left the house? Who announced that they were exiting? Were the male servants who held up the sheets allowed to see the women with their burqas on? Why them and not strangers passing by? Was it better if only a few, designated, lower-class male servants saw you than random strangers? In this story, we know that a woman's piety resides in her clothing, but does it also increase and decrease in relation to the number of men who see her? How often did these women leave the house, given the to-do associated with leaving: the covering, the calling of the carriage, the positioning of the carriage right outside the gate, the summoning of the male servants, the holding up of the sheets? Were these women even real? I'd never met anyone like them. But I suppose that was the point. Legends thrive as abstractions; they crumble, wither to the touch, as tangible, real people, as people who can say the wrong thing, who can disappoint.

Let's think a little more about the male servants. All societies that cloister segments of their population based on their gender or their wealth must also create a class of people who serve the needs of the cloistered. A lower, servile class. This makes pragmatic sense. If a segment of the population is just going to opt out of, or be prohibited from, full social existence, then others must facilitate, pay for, accommodate, compensate for all the interactions they can afford to forgo. You can insist that the women in your house remain cloistered when you can afford a house where women can wash the laundry inside and have a courtyard in which to hang it to dry; you can keep women inside the house gates when you can afford a house with a gate. Families who want their women concealed as they enter a covered carriage *need* servants.

The script I was raised with at home dictated that the more covered a woman, the more pious. At school, I learned the opposite. The less covered a woman, the more self-assured and independent; and the less covered women in general were, the more progressive, the more free 'we' were as a nation. The script at school cast the covered Muslim woman as oppressed. Muslim women who covered had no control over their lives. They needed saving. This was around the time of the first US incursion into Iraq, and the US government and media were colluding to emphasise the cultural 'otherness' of Muslims. How else could they write off the deaths of hundreds of thousands of innocent civilians as mere 'collateral damage'? Never mind that Iraq's dictator was secular and that Iraq had one of the highest female literacy rates in the world. Those were just irrelevant details. The script at school followed the media's narrative, and dismissed Muslim women who claimed to 'choose' the veil as having 'false consciousness'.

They think they want to wear the veil, but that's only because they're brainwashed!

Only uncovered women could have authentic consciousness. Only they had control over their bodies. Only they
were free and liberated.

Focusing on superficial things like clothing is a way of
covering up the deeper similarities, the shared systemic
oppressions, between 'us' and 'them'. It allows us to ignore
the fact that in North America women are valued less than
men. Literally. Women are paid less than men, our labour is
worth less. It allows us to turn a blind eye to the rates of
intimate partner violence here, the statistics on rape and
sexual assault, the lax repercussions for convicted rapists
and the murderers of women. Rather than seeing women's
lives as universally devalued differently everywhere – patriarchy is complex, sophisticated and pervasive – this script
pitted 'Muslim' women against 'Western' women, casting
Muslim women as particularly disadvantaged, as suffering a
qualitatively different kind of oppression.

The ironic thing about false consciousness is that there is
no way to escape the charge once it is levelled. I mean, if I
decided to remove the niqab because of racism and bigotry
and sexism, then wouldn't that also be an instance of 'false
consciousness'?

In this script, there was no place for me to honestly
discuss the circumstances under which I felt pressured to
wear niqab; that is, without portraying my mother as a
monster and me as a victim, without turning my story into
a site for a cosmological battle between 'Islam' and 'the
West'. Two categories that don't actually exist outside our

minds, categories that do not actually map on to any reality. What is the West? Or Islam? Where do they start, where do they end?

The scripts worked like veils, separating me from myself. They prevented me from seeing myself. Hearing myself. Feeling myself. There was no space for me to just be. I had to protect the very people I felt wronged by as the school script turned the tussle between me and my mother, which was universal and unspecial, into a cosmically significant one; it turned my mother's small and completely mundane tyrannies with a small 't', into Tyranny with a capital 'T'.

These opposing scripts left no room for me to live the life I was actually in, as I was experiencing it. Instead, I had to pick a script, a side. Which one would it be, would I choose the ideal femininity I learned at home, or the one held sacred at school? I picked the cult's script, my mother's script. Because that is where I lived, where I ate my food, where I slept. I came to sincerely believe that I wanted to wear niqab, that it had been my idea, and how sad that I lived in an ignorant society that couldn't make room for any other kind of femininity than the one held sacrosanct by second-wave feminism. I parroted the standard lines of the script that I was taught.

The niqab is liberating, it is a sign of my modesty. It protects me from commodification and sexualisation, which is what women's bodies are reduced to in the West. Degraded and humiliated. The niqab frees others to focus on me, as a person, on my ideas, rather than my body.

I repeated these lines, this script, even as I watched my niqab steal away all their meaning; people rarely heard me once they saw my niqab.

The truth is that once I faced all the hate just for wearing niqab, I could either adopt the niqab as my choice and tell others to fuck off, or take it off altogether. Each choice could easily be labelled 'false consciousness', each could be labelled oppression, and each could be labelled liberation, depending on who was doing the labelling. I chose to believe that wearing a niqab was my choice and came up with a narrative that made this true. Since I was going to wear niqab, I chose to label it an act of liberation, and picked the script in which I was a pious devotee, just trying to live my religion as best I could.

And at some point the niqab *did* become an act of devotion for me. Just because you make yourself believe something doesn't make your belief any less sincere. Belief forms freely, and breaks easily. That's the nature of belief. This is why we have rituals. Rituals, by their very nature, are repetitive. They are meant to remind us of what we believe, lest we forget. They form and re-form our beliefs, so that belief comes to follow action, rather than the other way around. This is true for praying five times a day and standing to sing the national anthem every morning. We are inducted into these rituals before we are old enough to know what they

mean, or why we are doing them, but over years of disciplined, persistent repetition, we learn what we are meant to
believe.

In my niqab, I knew I'd never fit in in Canada. There was
no point in trying. So I started dreaming my parents' dream.
The Dream of Return, a return to home. Except that I was
born in Canada, so I dreamed of leaving my country of
birth, which felt increasingly hostile, in search of a new
home, somewhere else. I began dreaming of living in a
Muslim country, in a Muslim world, surrounded by
Muslims. In a place where I'd be respected and valued.
Where I wouldn't be strange, where I wouldn't have to
explain myself, endlessly answering the same dumb fucking
questions. I dreamed of places I'd read about in books,
heard about in stories. Places like Syria, Yemen, Egypt,
Jordan. I wanted to go to the 'Muslim world', learn Islam
from 'real' Muslims. I was dreaming of a Muslim Homeland.

In so doing, I was marrying, mixing scripts, ones written
by Muslims dreaming of the golden age of Islam, and those
written by Orientalists – Europeans looking for the exotic
other against which to define themselves, measure themselves, orient themselves. These false narratives came
together to create a misguided impression in my mind. In
my imaginings, the Muslim world was a place in which
Islam was still pure, untainted by the West. I imagined

Bedouins riding camels over sand dunes, and men and women spending their free time studying and teaching Islam. These would be the most pious people, free to dress as they pleased, but always choosing the path of utmost modesty. I couldn't wait to join them, to be accepted by them. Maybe they'd marvel at how a girl raised in the clutches of the West could possibly choose to wear a niqab, maybe they would see my choice as strength, maybe they'd be so impressed.

When I finally got the chance to visit my Muslim Homeland, I was surprised and disappointed to find fully functioning cities and Muslims who practised Islam in varied and pluralistic ways. Damascus turned out to be the longest continually inhabited city in the world. It was complex and intricate, and there were no sand dunes in sight. Damascene women wore hijabs and jilbabs, and short skirts and T-shirts. The little fundamentalist that I was, I was scandalised by hijab-clad women smoking in restaurants and men hawking racy lingerie in the souk.

Thinking that maybe I'd missed the golden age of Islam in Damascus, I travelled to Yemen seeking a purer Islamic experience. I went to a little town where a community of Muslims aimed to emulate the earliest Muslim community. The women wore niqabs and jilbabs, dressed in black from head to toe. Now I was exactly where I wanted to be, in a town known for its religious devotion, surrounded by women wearing niqab. Finally. I was normative. This was the place I had been looking for all these years.

And I hated it. In this place there was nothing that set me apart; I was just another niqabi, or even worse, just another foreigner looking for an exotic experience. There was nothing to distinguish me from the women of the town in their black jilbabs and niqabs. Suddenly normal and unspecial, I went to my suitcase and pulled out a burgundy jilbab. The burgundy was almost shocking against everyone's black jilbabs, and, just like that, I was strange – special – again. Order was restored.

I realised in layers, over time, how my wearing niqab in Canada, even despite my evolving convictions, was never about Islam alone. It was also about individualism, and agency, and control over my body. Those ideas that white men came up with for themselves, during what they call the 'Enlightenment', when they thought that women were less human than men and that white people were the human-est of them all.

Sometimes we think we're being really clever and original in breaking a standard, boring script only to realise that we've fallen into another one without even knowing it. We can't actually write our own scripts, I think. Scripts are huge, they're bigger than any of us, they're formed by societies and cultures and religions over time.

The men whose ideas formed me to my very core, Muslim and Christian, brown and white, dead long ago

– none of them came up with their ideas with me in mind, a small, South Asian, Canadian, Muslim woman. And yet, their ideas, the scripts they devised, the writings they left behind surrounded me. I had to navigate through the complex web of their thoughts and opinions and feelings, to find a path that might feel free to me, that might allow me to escape the tangled maze they bequeathed us. But try as I might, I kept running into dead ends, retracing my steps, re-evaluating the truth of what I thought I knew. It's hard not to doubt myself, to think that, maybe, there's no way out at all.

Home, Again

People were just getting used to my niqab when I had to switch high schools. My parents moved from one suburb of Mississauga to another, forcing me to switch from a diverse high school to a mostly white high school. I had just spent a full year adjusting myself and others to my niqab, learning which parts of the school to avoid in order to minimise harassment, and then we moved.

My parents bought the four-bedroom house they now live in, on a corner lot. They were super excited and proud to be able to make this purchase. There were enough rooms in the house for their six children. After all those years of living in apartments with too many kids, saving up money and sending it to Pakistan, after trying to move back to Pakistan over and over again, to have finally scrimped and saved up the money to buy a house that their family could fit in, on just my father's blue-collar salary, was a spectacular achievement. The house was brand spanking new, the first to be built in a new development, so that the plots around us were empty and muddy, where, eventually, we would watch tractors dig out basements, mixer trucks pour in cement, churning it like it was ice-cream, and men in hats and overalls put up two-by-fours that would form the skeletons of the houses before dressing them up in brick. If the owners were fancy, they might put up some stonework on the facade. The neighbourhood didn't have complete sidewalks yet – we'd watch those get poured too. And the trees would be planted later, once the houses were up. Tiny little saplings. My young, unbelieving eyes thought it impossible that these young saplings could grow into full, thick, mature trees. But they have, for everything that lives ages, fills in and out before it withers, grows small and dies.

When we moved into our house, the giant lot across the way was still a landfill piled high with garbage, birds picking away at it, the smell of rot and general foulness drifting our way when the wind blew in a certain direction. We'd go rummaging in the lot adjacent to the landfill, which was full of short, sometimes brown, sometimes green scrub, searching for rocks. Beautiful, sparkly, multicoloured rocks, rocks upon which rainbows had made an impression, leaving behind streaks of pink and red and orange mixing in with the grey, making even the grey look dazzling. We'd pocket these rocks and bring them home, playing with them instead of watching TV or playing video games, because we were allowed neither. It was a group activity, this collecting of rocks, rubbing off dirt to inspect them, discovering them, showing them to each other, sometimes marvelling and sometimes jealous at what a sibling had found. We'd team up together when we found a big rock, lugging it home together, carrying it in turns, maybe one or two or three at a time, feeling a great sense of accomplishment at bringing it into our yard. There were free treasures across the street, just sitting there, waiting to be discovered, and with a little bit of effort they could be ours.

Because the house was new, my parents had some input on its details. They got to pick a floor plan. They agonised over the colour of the brick that would adorn the house, feeling that the decision would make a statement about them as people. Eventually, they settled on a neutral sand. They fretted over the colour of the carpet as well, in the end picking a rose pink. And they chose an off-white paint for the walls, but we repainted them many times together, as a family, over the years. Eventually, each room in the house would have its own colour, lavender purple in my brother's room, blue in my sister's room, floral cut-outs decorating the yellow kitchen. And my father installed long tube lights, like you find in office buildings, in our bedrooms, so we'd have plenty of light and save money on electricity at the same time. Win-win.

The basement of the house was unfinished when we first moved in, but was quickly turned into a living space by my older brother, then an undergraduate. He installed a pantry, a kitchenette, two bedrooms and a living room in the basement. My mother taught Qur'an classes down there and many families in transition lived there over the years, my parents happily offering them the extra space in the house, with pride, grateful to be able to provide this help to those in need. My parents had relied on the kindness of strangers and friends while in transition themselves; they stayed in community members' basements with their children while sorting out their affairs, especially when returning from failed resettlement trips to Pakistan. Now, they were honoured to be able to treat others with the kindness that had sustained them when they were in need.

And they continued receiving generosity from their community too. One summer, when I was an undergraduate at the University of Toronto, I planned a cross-country trip for us. The trip was a consolation of sorts. My older brother was getting married in Pakistan – my mother had arranged the marriage and was present for the wedding. But we couldn't afford a trip to Pakistan for the whole family – we'd just been there last year for my sister's wedding. So, I convinced my father that while my brother was getting married, those of us who couldn't go should take a cross-country road trip instead. My plan was low key and low cost, with us mostly camping in national parks along the way. When we arrived in a city at night, without a national park nearby and in desperate need of a shower, we rented a motel room. My dad would rent one room for himself and we would all sneak in through the back stairs. We did that a few times. But before it came to that, my father would insist on stopping by a phone booth – at that time, phone booths were still a thing – to cold-call people with South Asian and Muslim-sounding names. He'd look through the local phone book in the booth, call the numbers attached to friendly-sounding names, and, if they answered, he'd say, *Assalamu 'alaikum! We're Muslim, in town for the night, can we stay with you?*

We'd be in the car, cringing. But sure enough, the community came through. We spent several nights with total strangers who fed us home-cooked meals and offered us clean beds.

In our own home, there was plenty of room for all of us. My parents got the largest bedroom, with an en-suite bathroom, and the three remaining bedrooms were divided between the six of us. The boys were together in the room above the garage with an en-suite bathroom of their own. This room was closest to the front of the house, the most public; if you opened the curtains, you could be seen from the street. The girls would have been too exposed in that room. So the girls split up the two rooms in the centre of the house, playing musical chairs over the years, changing the algorithm by which rooms were divided as some of us got married and others moved away for school. For most of my time there, the four daughters shared the most central bathroom of the house, the one in the hallway. The wooden wicker basket in that bathroom was procured from a yard sale, and contained the cloth rags for catching our menstrual blood and for cutting into thin strips for waxing off our hair. When we washed and hung the menstrual rags to dry over the shower rod, we didn't have to explain ourselves or be ashamed of our bodies. We spent a lot of time in that bathroom. We'd go in there to talk shit about our parents or each other. We'd leave the water running so we wouldn't be overheard. It was a real communal place, that bathroom.

Now, my parents' bedroom is my mother's. One of the girls' rooms is my father's, and he uses the girls' bathroom.

And the boys' room is a guest suite for whoever – family or friend – might be visiting. And the landfill across the way is a golf course.

Back to high school. Moving from Applewood Heights, where brown people were plentiful enough to form cliques, to Streetsville Secondary, where there were only a handful of brown people scattered across the grade levels, was rough. I had to teach a whole new group of white people how to deal with a niqabi, which is to say, I had to teach them how to treat me as if I were human. I had to teach them that I could speak English, and that a cloth did not get in the way of my words, or my thoughts. Cloth never does.

I didn't have a lot of Muslim friends in school, and there were a few reasons for this. First, there weren't a lot of Muslims to begin with. Second, Muslims didn't like that I wore a niqab; they didn't see it as Islamic and didn't want to be associated with my brand of Islam. Third, I was a bit of a pill. I was an incessant evangelist, preaching to Muslims about how they could be better Muslims – *start wearing hijab, stop wearing Western clothing, read more Qur'an, stop having boyfriends, stop spending time with non-Muslims*. I can hardly blame them for not wanting to be around me.

In both high schools, I was harassed and bullied for wearing niqab. It was much worse at Streetsville than it was at Applewood Heights. And there was a crucial difference between the bullies at the two schools. It was mostly non-Muslim white boys who harassed me at Applewood Heights while the Muslims there gave me a wide berth, but in Streetsville, the white kids were joined in their bullying by a light-skinned Pakistani Muslim boy. He was my most relentless bully and he was everywhere. I couldn't avoid him if I tried. I'd always run into him. He would call me names – *terrorist, ninja, retard* – he'd fake me out pretending to hit me, he'd make faces and stick his tongue out, he'd bang lockers really hard when walking by me, making me jump at the sudden loud sound, which threatened of violence. He could have hit me just as easily. He terrorised me in the school hallways. He really hated me. And he was Muslim and I knew his family – we'd known each other as children – but I didn't know if he knew who I was, or if he knew that I knew who he was, or if he cared either way. I didn't complain about him to my parents because I was afraid that if he got in trouble at home, things would only get worse at school. The physical discipline, which is to say, the physical abuse of children, is quite common. Some families brag about how they keep their children in line with violence, while others are quieter about it. My bully's family was known for using violence to keep their children 'straight'.

And I couldn't bring myself to complain about him at school, because I felt like I'd be betraying Muslims if he got in trouble. So I just lived with it, through all my years at Streetsville. It never got worse, but it never got better either.

A few years out of high school, my bully landed in the hospital after getting stabbed in a knife fight. My brother went to see him soon after. He said to my brother, *I want to apologise to your sister. I made her life hell in high school. I feel really bad about that.*

Turns out he knew me the whole time.

My only Muslim friends in high school were a couple of girls, one Turkish and one Moroccan, both of whom I thought couldn't resist my mix of wisdom and wit, but now realise they were most likely attracted to my intolerant, toxic religiosity powered by guilt and shame. It was compelling for them because they were looking for boundaries. In their own way, each of them was in free fall, and my narrow, restricted but completely predictable, boring and safe rules for life, which disallowed me from doing most things, appealed to them. Imagine if they could be saved from the pain and confusion of their growing, hormone-riddled bodies by just opting out of all experimentation and growth? In reality, I would have switched places with either of them in a heartbeat, but since I couldn't, I settled into the righteous superiority my lacklustre lifestyle afforded me, happy also to have their company to lighten my loneliness. During lunch breaks, I would teach them to read the Qur'an, starting from a primer, going through the Arabic alphabet, teaching them the vowels, and then how to connect letters

into words. I'd hold forth on the importance of Islam and
the necessity to resist the corrupting influences of the West,
parroting whichever VHS tape I'd watched of Mark
Hanson, a white man who went by the name Hamza Yusuf,
that weekend.

During my entire high school career, I had two white
friends, Robert and Noah. Both were male. Both were
intrigued by my niqab, the exoticism and mystery of it. Both
admired it to some degree, which likely means they had
certain conservative and patriarchal leanings. Both enjoyed
talking endlessly about religion. I met Noah in English class,
and Robert in Calculus. At some point, I had a crush on
both.

Noah was Italian and had thick, floppy hair that fell over
the side of his face. One time, when I was sitting in class,
reading, waiting for class to begin, he came up behind me,
peered over my shoulder to see what I was reading and
brought his face close enough to mine that his hair touched
my temple, just by my eye, where skin was exposed through
the slit in my niqab. I remember being thrilled and stunned
by this small gesture that likely meant nothing to Noah but
too much to me. The intimacy, his hair touching my skin,
was exhilarating. So too was his willingness to come close, to
treat me like a friend, to not treat me differently because of
my niqab, to treat me like a person, a real person. More
than two decades later, I still remember the moment vividly.
Which, in some ways, makes the memory painful because it
makes me see just how alienated and lonely I felt, that a

gesture as small as that could mean so much. When I came to school one day and told him that I'd gotten engaged, and that my parents had arranged it, and that I was okay with it, he asked, *Does he know how smart you are?*

I hadn't even spoken to my fiancé yet, so probably not.

Robert was in my thirteenth-grade Calculus class – we had thirteen grades back then. I hated calculus but I liked going to class because Robert was there. He was tall and white and Catholic. I'd chat with him before class while I waited outside the portable for Ms Figuredo to let us into the classroom, holding an embroidery hoop in one hand and a needle in the other, as I cross-stitched little flowers for a cushion. I was trying to keep myself from wasting time, learning some real life skills, like cross-stitching rather than calculus. I'm pretty sure I tried converting Robert to Islam, I know I gave him a copy of Yusuf Ali's translation of the Qur'an. Yusuf Ali was a British-Indian barrister, an Anglophile with two failed marriages to white women, who translated the Qur'an into super snobby British English. Robert didn't convert, but we bonded over our shared conservative values.

I also hung out with the goth kids in high school. They let me hover around them; they smoked whatever they were smoking and I'd just stand around. We'd talk about capitalism and 'the machine'. They grudgingly admired me because I was more countercultural than they were, with my niqab and all. But we didn't have very much in common beyond the fact that we weren't trying to conform to dominant beauty standards. Secretly, I wished I was excelling at conformity, but since I didn't stand a chance in hell at winning at that game, I had to settle with winning at nonconformity. I thought I might have something in common with one of them in particular, a tall, shaggy-haired white guy in a long black trench coat and military boots. We lamented 'society' together, and 'consumer culture' and 'the media'. But then he told me that Jeffery Dahmer was his hero, and I had to stop talking to him.

My siblings and I were discouraged from having non-Muslim friends. They weren't good for our faith because they didn't share it. Procedurally, it was difficult to have non-Muslim friends anyway because we couldn't hang out after school. When we were not doing schoolwork, my mother had us studying the Qur'an, biographies of the Prophet Muhammad, listening to religious lectures and debates, and working our way through a curriculum for Urdu studies. If friends came to visit, they were not allowed to wear shorts, or dresses, or sleeveless shirts. The girls were asked if they'd wear hijab while in the house. We couldn't hang out in our rooms unsupervised. One of my mother's foundational rules was, *There is no privacy in this house.* Privacy was white. We were not white. We did not need privacy.

We were all up in each other's business, we were taught to watch one another, watch over each other and report back if one of us broke the rules. You know, for the good of everyone. This made it tough to have male friends at school, even for the duration of the school day. I couldn't have lunch with a male friend because I always had a sibling in school with me. When I started ninth grade, my older sister was in twelfth grade. After that, my younger brother was always in high school with me. It was reported to my mom when the Muslim kid who lived across the street said *hi* to me a few times on the bus.

She talks to boys, says hi *to Naveed all the time.*

That was the end of that. I had to ignore Naveed and his kind overtures thereafter. And I adapted, making sure that all my conversations with boys happened immediately before, during, or immediately after class, so I wouldn't be seen talking to them.

Was I miserable? Of course I was. I dreamed of killing myself. I tried cutting my wrists with an X-acto knife. It hurt too much and I felt like a coward for not being able to go deeper. I went to see a school therapist about this once. The white woman with short brown hair who examined me was unperturbed and uncaring about my desire to kill myself. She didn't believe me.

If you're not going deep, it probably means you're not suicidal, she declared.

My mother once noticed the cuts on my wrist, which were usually easily hidden by the long sleeves I always wore.

What's that? she asked.

Oh, a paper cut, I answered.

Unbelievable answer that she was quick to accept. She didn't ask how I got multiple paper cuts on my wrists. The one time she shouldn't have respected my privacy, she did.

Like any teenager, my high school years were fraught with angst and existential crises, but they were also full of richness and complexity. Yes, I lived with a difficult set of entirely constructed and unnecessary rules. It would have been hard enough to be a brown, South Asian girl in a primarily white high school in Canada. Adding the layers of fundamentalist Islam and a conservative culture around gender made things exponentially more challenging. But fundamentalist Islam also made me feel like I belonged to something bigger. It staved off my experiences with racism, which I only really fully encountered in all its ugliness once I removed my niqab and hijab, exposing my brown skin to the world. Hyperperforming my identity as a Muslim cushioned me from blatant racism, or at least redirected it to Islamophobia, for a little while. And my Muslim identity was an important part of my self-understanding. I believed Islam was special and I felt lucky to be Muslim. I still do.

I have warm feelings about my life in that house in Mississauga. For a few years, we were all there, in that house, together. The six of us children and our parents. It was a special time. We laughed really hard, watched Ahmed Deedat debates. We played badminton in the backyard, sometimes in the early morning light, right after Fajr, with the wet dew tickling our feet, and other times in the evening, as the sun set. We prayed in the yard, or in the house, together as a family. My mother cooked us parathas for breakfast, the smell of frying butter, or margarine or Crisco filling the house. We would dip the parathas in big bowls of yogurt which my mother or father made in a huge CorningWare donga, wrapped up in a blanket, like a cosy little baby. Store-made yogurt was for stupid people who didn't know they could make better yogurt at home. We were loud and raucous in that house, it was encouraged, a virtue, it was praised as 'ronak'. We would eat ketchup chips, pouring them into a bowl and then sitting in a circle eating them, leaving some at the end for our youngest sister, who was a slow eater. We ate tubs of ice-cream, especially Neapolitan, piling the vanilla and strawberry and chocolate so high in the cones the stack teetered. I could pile ice-cream really high on a cone and so was in great demand at ice-cream time. We engaged in the regular cruelties of children, trying to exclude one or another from our games. Once, my brother and I tied my younger sister to a fence with skipping ropes so we could play on our own. We might have left her there for hours. Forgive me, dear.

When our parents went out for a mosque event or a wedding or a dinner party, we'd beg to be allowed to stay home to do homework. But as soon as they left, we'd rush to their bedroom, which housed the only TV, and watch clandestinely. My parents purchased this TV soon after moving into the house for the purpose of 'knowledge' – which included the news and video lectures of Israr Ahmed, or Mark Hanson, or Ahmed Deedat. When our parents left us alone in the house, we'd watch TV shows in their bedroom, at a low volume, standing close to the TV, making one person a lookout to warn us of the sound of wheels turning into the driveway, signalling our parents' return. At that sound, we'd shout, *They're home!* And we'd scramble to our rooms, make like we'd been reading or writing quietly the whole time. It is like that – secretly, at low volume, standing huddled together – that we watched whatever happened to be on TV at the time. *Invasion of the Body Snatchers*. Alfred Hitchcock's *The Birds*. *Murphy Brown*. *Friends*.

We had hundreds of people come through the house on Eid, when friends and friends of friends would drop by our 'open house' all day long, unannounced. My mother would cook a huge pot of her famous haleem, which we'd serve with bagels, and I'd make potato salad with macaroni and shredded carrots and several jars of mayonnaise. We raised chickens and roosters in our backyard so we could have meat that was both halal, which is to say slaughtered correctly, and tayyib, as in pure. When the neighbours complained about the racket the roosters made at daybreak, I argued with the weary-looking forty-something city official who came by to tell us to get rid of the birds. When he insisted that we comply, I said, *Well, if I have to change my behaviour for a noise complaint, then you should change your behaviour too. I have a noise complaint about the airplanes that fly over the house every twenty minutes. Change the flight routes, because the noise is disturbing me!*

Already, I was asking, *Whose comfort matters?*

And picking up on the answer, *Not yours!*

We churned butter, old school, with unpasteurised milk my father picked up from a local farm, sitting on a piri, rubbing the wooden handle of the churn between our palms, as the flat wooden head swirled the unpasteurised milk around the clay pot, till we ended up with soft, white, fluffy, buttery cream on top. Then we'd scoop it out, toast a wholewheat slice from an expired but perfectly good loaf of bread, spread the heavenly cream on top, sprinkle it with coarse sugar and eat it with lightly salted, sugary chai as a snack.

I'd be lying if I didn't say that, sometimes, I desperately miss those times.

Extremism

A few years ago I found myself at a meeting, organised by Religious Studies' academics, with representatives from the FBI. Well, I didn't just find myself there. I was invited and I accepted. I felt conflicted about going, and now I know that I probably didn't need to be there. The meeting was held at Harvard University and, unsurprisingly, the majority of the people in the room were white. We had a fancy lunch in an old-timey room, with linen sheets covering circular tables. Academics and FBI agents were sprinkled across the tables. I was the only person of colour at our table. We skipped from topic to topic as we ate. I watched my colleagues pitch themselves to the FBI, *My research could be useful to you because I work on Izlaam,* or some version of that.

The topic of 'extremism' didn't take long to come up, and when it did, my ears perked up. I wondered whether the FBI was taking white supremacist groups seriously when thinking about extremism and, if so, how they were doing that. Several agents said, *Yes, yes, of course we take this seriously.* And then one agent said, *Actually, we take domestic terrorism very seriously, and right now we're noticing a sharp rise in 'Black Identity Extremism'.* I was floored. I had never heard about this before, so I asked some questions, the answers to which clarified that I had not misunderstood. The FBI was worried about the rise of groups like Black Lives Matter that were protesting state institutions and galvanising communities at the grassroots level. The Bureau's position was that those calling for racial justice in the wake of widespread, documented cases of police brutality were taking part in an 'extremist' discourse.

Extremism is one of those words that does a lot of work but is somehow empty of meaning. It is a word that is heavy with moral censure, easily manipulated by opportunistic politics. It is a word that is necessarily vague and hazy; in order for it to have endlessly varied uses, it must resist a fixed meaning. So its meaning is always fluid and subjective, and the way it is used gives us insight into what its user perceives as dangerous or threatening to their own interests. Whenever I hear the word 'extreme' or 'extremist' used to describe an idea or a person, I wonder, *What work is this word doing for you? How are you positioned, in relation to this extremism? How do you benefit from the demonisation of this person, group or idea?*

For much of my life, I have been accused of being an 'extremist' by different people with various bones to pick. On one end of the spectrum, some Muslims and non-Muslims saw my niqab as signalling my extremist tendencies, and on the other end of the spectrum, some Muslims and non-Muslims view my commitment to feminism as extremist. Of course, I do not believe that I am an extremist. I support the right of women to wear whatever they want, without interference from the state, and I believe that humans, regardless of gender, have equal dignity and that their dignity isn't inherently worth more than that of non-human animals and plants. I don't think any of these beliefs make me an extremist. In fact, from my standpoint, you could just as well describe secular fanaticism, unfettered capitalism, intolerance of the niqab, or patriarchy (valuing the lives and worth of non-men less than those of men) as 'extreme'.

'Extreme' is a label we put on behaviours and ideas that deviate from what we consider the 'norm', what is usual, ordinary, customary, what is called 'urf in legal texts, what is considered ma'ruf. But what if the norm is monstrous, oppressive, cruel? What if the norm is genocidal? What if the norm turns lives into commodities, to be bought and sold; what if the norm values, say, money above all else, above the earth herself? Where, then, do we place the extremes?

What I'm saying is, it can be useful to pay attention to how the word 'extreme' is used around you. It is a word that revolves around us all the time, defining the boundaries of acceptable behaviour, threatening dire consequences if we dare step out of line, ask the wrong questions, or just advocate for ourselves.

I often wonder if Tanzeem was an 'extremist' organisation. I think it is fair to call it a fundamentalist group, since Israr Ahmed himself adopted the title 'fundamentalist' with pride. But he didn't consider himself an extremist; though, of course, no one considers themselves to be extremist. Just like no one believes themselves to be racist or sexist; well, almost no one. Israr Ahmed saw 'the West' as extreme, as deviating from the norms set by God. He especially found Western education threatening: universities, he said, were the equivalent of 'training camps', where we were brainwashed by the West. Dr Israr Ahmed believed that he had somehow, miraculously, managed to escape the corrupting influences of 'the West' during his own medical education by engaging with the 'Western' part of the sciences as little as possible, and was now trying to save us from corruption through the tired and highly ineffectual method of abstinence.

Beware the one who seeks to save you on the assumption of his own exceptionalism.

Israr Ahmed preached a vision of the world where 'the West' was the enemy of 'Islam', as though the two were separate and distinct entities. This narrative, commonly known as the 'clash of civilisations' and attributed to Samuel Huntington, was hardly original. Nor is it original that an old idea is now attributed to a living white man. The narrative long predates Huntington; it has existed for centuries, and has been propagated by all sides. It is a simplistic and stupid idea. It is a cop-out. It allows us to point fingers at the 'essential' nature of others and avoid self-critical scrutiny. But, as my mother likes to say, if you point your finger at someone, three of your fingers point back at you. No one has an 'essential' nature, not even a single person. We transform and are created anew by our circumstances all the time. Anytime people start talking about the essential nature of people, you know they're full of shit.

So, I guess the primary ideas of Tanzeem – the clash of civilisations narrative, the aspirations for a khilafa, the patriarchy of it all – taken together might sound extreme. But Tanzeem was avowedly anti-violence. It took seriously the Qur'anic command, *kuffu aydiyakum*, 'tie your hands', even in the face of violence, not even allowing its members to fight back in self-defence. If someone has extreme views but isn't a violent threat, do we consider them extremists? What is the difference between an extremist and an idealist? Is the difference violence? Or the threat of violence? Do we only label people extremists when we're scared of them and their ideas?

By the time I got to university, I had bought into the clash of civilisations narrative hook, line and sinker; especially so because it was validated for me by the white man himself. The white man, in this case, was an American convert to Islam who became a popular Muslim preacher. His name was, well, let's just call him John Doe. Whatever his birth name, when he converted to Islam, Doe took Arabic first and last names. One of those names was 'Yusuf'. Yusuf is the Arabic name for the prophet Joseph, who is known in Islam as the most beautiful man to have ever existed. When the women of Egypt whispered judgemental gossip about the noblewoman Zulaykha trying to seduce Yusuf, who was her servant at the time, her defence was simply to let them see him. She knew that once they saw him, the women would understand that they would have done the same, given the opportunity. To set the scene, she invited the women over, set tables piled high with fruit and gave each of them a knife, supposedly for cutting the fruit. Then she asked Yusuf to walk through the room, you know, super casual. When they saw him, the women were so taken by his beauty, they cut their own hands instead of the fruit; so distracted were they by his gorgeousness, they didn't feel the knives cutting into their own flesh, spilling their own blood. 'Yusuf' is a remarkably popular name among white male converts who adopt an Arabic name to signify their conversion to Islam, turning their conversion into a kind of birth. It is one thing for a mother to look at her newborn child and think, *You are so beautiful, I will name you Yusuf.* It's quite another for a grown man to think, *I am so hot, I must be a Yusuf.*

To emphasise his authority and transformation, John Doe appropriated an 'Islamic' identity to go with his new name. Doe understood 'Muslim' as 'Arab' and dressed himself like the Arabs of his imagination, wearing long, flowing white robes and an imama wrapped around his head. He even spoke with a hint of an Arab accent, and peppered his sentences with over-pronounced Arabic words, really playing up the *'ayn*s and *qaf*s and *kha*s. His performance of 'Muslimness' worked, because he was one of the few people allowed into our home, which is how my parents thought of TV. Watching people on TV, through videos or DVDs or regular programming, was like inviting them into your living room. My parents were extremely selective about whose lectures we could listen to, and Doe made the cut, mostly because his views aligned with the ideology of Tanzeem. His message wasn't threatening; in fact, he confirmed almost everything Israr Ahmed preached.

There were a lot of similarities between Doe and Israr Ahmed. Israr Ahmed was trained as a medical doctor, and Doe was trained as a nurse. Like Israr Ahmed, Doe considered himself an Islamic scholar without having formal seminary training. Also like Israr Ahmed, Doe believed that he had somehow, miraculously, managed to escape the corrupting influences of 'the West', despite being a white man born, raised and educated in this very same 'West'. In line with Tanzeemi ideology, Doe endorsed the clash of civilisations narrative, casting 'the West' and 'Islam' as enemies of each other, and himself as the enlightened émigré, the one who crossed over, saw it all, saw the truth, as the one who adopted the light of Islam and rejected the darknesses of the West, the one who had somehow escaped and expunged 'the West' from his white male self. And now, he warned rooms full of mostly brown and black Muslims of the perils of 'the 'West', its philosophy, its education, its general moral depravity.

Beware the one who seeks to save you on the assumption of his own exceptionalism.

Doe espoused a patriarchal version of Islam as the only authentic Islam. A patriarchal Islam is appealing to a good deal of conservative white men. It offers them religious sanction and a righteous platform from which to spew toxic patriarchal rhetoric; rhetoric that is inescapably misogynistic, homophobic, and promotes hierarchies in which they are the chosen ones. Doe ferociously defended patriarchal Islam, often responding with anger and derisiveness to anything or anyone, real or imagined, who challenged him. He jumped from topic to topic, without rhyme or reason, yelling about one thing or another. He made Israr Ahmed look like a rational, organised thinker. As a teenager, I thrilled at his self-righteous incoherence, mistaking his anger for passion, his verbosity for intelligence, his rants for lectures.

It is difficult to describe his 'philosophy' per se. My memories of his talks are impressionistic. I remember specific things that upset him. Doe found homosexuality disgusting and it angered him that homosexuals might have legal rights. He was obsessed with pornography. He saw it as an urgently pressing problem and warned against its damaging physiological effects; apparently it causes impotence. He blamed immigrants for their experiences of racism in North America and Europe, originally, before 9/11, blaming them for trying too hard to be white and Western when they'd obviously never be accepted. Then later, after 9/11, he blamed immigrants for failing to properly assimilate and for hanging on to their cultural baggage. Following a long American tradition, he blamed racial inequality in the United States on the breakdown of the 'black family'. When it was brought to his attention that this was a racist claim that blamed the victims of structural inequality for suffering in a system designed to oppress them, he leaned on classic white tactics to defend himself; he cried, and then claimed he couldn't be racist because his mother once had a black boyfriend.

Unsurprisingly, given his commitment to a patriarchal Islam, Doe detested Muslim feminists. Muslim feminists challenged the very legitimacy of patriarchal Islam, which jeopardised Doe; they threatened to rip from him the mantle of his tenuously crafted authority. Given that a great deal of Muslim feminist scholarship is produced in universities, Doe described universities as institutions of higher brainwashing. In general, he confirmed all the things I had learned from Israr Ahmed. His lectures were just angrier and more visceral, which made them more fun to watch.

Not all religious conversions are cultural appropriations, but there are some that definitely feel like they are. I'm wary of white converts who become 'experts' on Islam, make money off their conversions, who quickly and easily take positions of leadership as though a 1,400-year-old community was just waiting for them to come along and lead us to the promised land. When I think of John Doe, it is difficult for me to not think about Rachel Dolezal. They're both white people trading on their assumed identities – religious and racial – in a way that increases their social capital; their careers are built on their conversion. Who would even know his name if he hadn't converted to Islam?

And I wonder too, did he change his name legally, like on his driver's licence? Is he his Muslim name when he's condescending to us, but John Doe when he gets pulled over by the cops?

Anyways, you get the point. The guy was an embodiment of the colonial legacy, as in a white man who converted to our religion, then claimed expertise on us, then assumed positions of authority over us, and now had the audacity to behave as an arbiter of 'real' and 'cultural' Islam, separating it away from corrupting influences. His preachings aligned with all the fundamentalist ideas I had been raised with, but they were especially potent in him, because in him they were packaged in an imperious white body. White supremacy upon patriarchy. Misogyny and homophobia and racism, each building on the other.

Like the overwhelming darknesses of the deep ocean, where waves cover waves and are covered in turn by clouds. Darknesses one upon the other. When he holds out his hand, he cannot see it. There is no light for the one whom God has made no light.

أو كظلمـت فى بحر لجى يغشه موج من فوقه موج من فوقه سحاب ظلمـت بعضها فوق بعض إذا أخرج يده لم يكد يرها ومن لم يجعل الله له نورا فما له من نور﴿۟﴾

Like other South Asians, descendants of a colonised people who have internalised the colonialists' view of whiteness as superior, I found validation and beauty in white people. They were all Yusufs to me. I was obsessed with John Doe. I loved him. I believed the light of God radiated from his face, though that was more likely the camera light reflecting off his forehead. I loved his severity. I was sure that he'd be impressed by me, proud of me, with my niqab and all, resisting assimilation, being Muslim first, spurning 'the West' by not wearing Western clothing. I watched his videos over and over again. Got high off his bitchy zingers.

Doe talked longingly and incessantly about the time he spent learning Islam from 'real' Muslims in the Middle East and Africa. He was never specific about the details of this learning. But he talked all the time about his time among the 'Bedouins' in the desert, the most 'authentic' humans he'd ever met. He exoticised the shit out of these people, painting a perfect Orientalist picture for his followers. I was mesmerised by his tales. I too wanted to learn Islam from 'real' Muslims, Bedouins in the desert. Why would I study science or engineering when I could be studying Islam?

So, when it came time to apply for university, I decided against it. This was the olden days, when your high school provided you with applications for university and college (two different things in Canada) and you filled them out by hand to be submitted by your school. When I didn't turn in any applications, my teacher asked me why.

Oh, I'm not going to university.

Why not? You're bright, you'd do well.

Well, I want to learn Islam and it doesn't make sense to do that at a Western university. Besides, universities are institutions of higher brainwashing.

I'd learned that from Doe. My teacher was bewildered. I mean, what do you say to that?

I guess some of my teachers discussed my decision among themselves, because another teacher, Ms Figuredo, confronted me shortly thereafter. She was Caribbean of South Asian heritage, wore leather boots and knee-length skirts to class, and was married to a white Italian man. Rumour had it she was Muslim and her husband was not. Steeped as I was in a patriarchal version of Islam, I found this news to be morally and ethically troubling. See, according to a patriarchal Islam (and may I remind you, there is a strong and thriving egalitarian Islam), Muslim men are allowed to marry Christian and Jewish women, but Muslim women are restricted to Muslim men. The assumption here is that children will take the religion of the dominant parent, which, big surprise, is presumed to be the father. Ms Figuredo's marriage posed a challenge for me. Did she not worry that her marriage was invalid? Wasn't she worried about her children's faith? I adored her and wanted to save her. What if she didn't know of the metaphysical danger she was in? I'd never met a secular Muslim before, or I was in denial about having met any, so I couldn't fathom that perhaps Ms Figuredo did not care about my Islamic perspective on her marriage.

While I was trying to build up the courage to save Ms Figuredo, she saved me. She cornered me in the hallway between classes, *I heard you're not going to apply to university.*

Yeah, I said and parroted the lines I'd said to the other teacher, about learning Islam from 'real' Muslims and the bit about universities being a form of 'higher brainwashing'. In retrospect, I don't even know what that means. I must have sounded high – *Dude, I wanna learn Islam from, like, you know, real Muslims.*

Well, she bargained, *could you do me a favour? Please just apply? You don't have to go if you get in.*

Sure, I said.

That sounded reasonable enough. It couldn't hurt to apply. Then she narrowed her eyes at me, *And if you don't go, you're a waste of brains.*

Before I could respond, she spun around and walked off. I stood there for a few seconds, in my rose pink niqab, absorbing what she had just said.

I applied to three universities – Toronto, Queens and Waterloo. I got into all three. I was in Pakistan when I heard. We were there for my sister's wedding. My dad, who had returned to Canada immediately after the wedding, mailed the acceptance letters and the course catalogues to Pakistan.

I remember sitting with the course catalogues in my mother's childhood home, once owned by her father, and now by her brothers. I sat in the courtyard, on a chaar-pai, in the same courtyard and perhaps the same chaar-pai that supported my grandfather's dead body. I sat in that courtyard, in a house that had belonged to our family for only one generation, having been claimed when they fled from India, leaving behind their own haveli, their own interconnected homes, their land, their animals. They claimed this house, a house that belonged to another Punjabi family, a Hindu or a Sikh family.

I pulled out the course catalogues and felt their weight in my hands. I flipped despondently through them, uninterested in their contents. I wanted to go to Queens, but only because the name appealed to me as a good colonial subject. I decided to go to the University of Toronto – my older siblings had gone there, and I could commute from home. In truth, there wasn't much of a choice, since I wasn't going to be allowed to live away from home anyway.

I signed up to be a student at the University of Toronto's Victoria College – again, because I was drawn to the name, chained to my history. It's funny; I was worried about being brainwashed at university, but I registered at Victoria College because I liked the sound of the Queen's name. *Too late*, I think now, looking back, *you were already brainwashed, kiddo!* I 'liked' the sound of the name of a woman who colonised my homeland, stole its resources, pitted my ancestors one against the other, so that the homeland would be split asunder, so that my parents' families would have to flee the homes they had lived in for generations, the land they'd lived and died on for centuries, thus displacing my parents not just once, from India to Pakistan but a second time, from Pakistan to Canada: Canada, another country of which she made herself the Queen, colonised by her emissaries, a country where the Indigenous population would fare worse than my own because the settler colonialists would never leave. And despite all this, when registering for university and looking at the list of colleges I could choose from – New College, St Michael's College, Woodsworth College – I chose Victoria because it sounded romantic and whimsical and idyllic, rather than murderous and ruthless and cursed. My 'liking' the name, that was the sign, the tell of a brain already thoroughly washed. I 'liked' that name, while sitting in the courtyard of a house I was only in because of the fucking Queen and her sense of entitlement.

If extremism is a feeling of superiority, a sense of exceptionalism so complete that you imagine you have the right to dominate everyone and everything around you, and you are willing to destroy the earth, poison the land and kill human and non-human animals to achieve your goals, then Queen Victoria was most definitely an extremist.

But I didn't understand all of that back then. I thought of my brain not so much washed as pure, and to keep it that way while in university I decided to start out part-time and take only two classes my first year: Arabic, since I figured you couldn't get brainwashed in a language class, and 'Global Politics', taught by the famed political scientist Janice Stein, in which I would be on high alert for brainwashing. My parents weren't really involved in any of these decisions. When my older brother went to university, his course selection was a family affair, my mother poring over the course catalogue with him, my parents debating which courses would be best. With me, they didn't worry so much. I'd be married soon anyway, I didn't really need the education.

Though it is worth noting that I didn't have to fight for an education either. My parents supported my education, they considered it a perfectly acceptable pursuit while I waited to get married, they even paid for my undergraduate degree. I got scholarships for the master's and doctoral degrees. And when it came time for my doctoral studies at New York University, even though my parents were not happy about me moving to New York City by myself, my older sister drove me down to my new apartment, with her two kids in tow, the van full of my belongings. What I'm saying is, it wasn't just me against the world.

Still, I made all these decisions on a whim, sitting alone in a courtyard in Gujranwala, in the same house in which, just a few decades earlier, my grandfather decided it was more important for my mother to care for her own grandfather than it was for her to get an education – just outside the room where she *cried without end* for the opportunity she lost, the things she would never learn and the future she would never have.

I attended the downtown campus of the University of Toronto – a massive, sprawling city within a city. I would commute in from Mississauga on a big yellow school bus operated by the university just for its suburban students. The bus sped along Mississauga Road, which is where the wealthiest people in Mississauga lived. Unsurprisingly, it was also one of the whitest parts of town. It was lined with expensive and gaudy, mostly enormous houses in all different styles, old and new, some with elaborate golden gates, or high impenetrable hedges, or long driveways with multiple fancy cars. Sometimes there were grand houses set back on sprawling lawns, as if this were the English countryside rather than the suburbs of Toronto. The bus would rumble down Mississauga Road, take the on-ramp to the Queen Elizabeth Highway, and then merge on to the Gardiner Expressway, racing past the new buildings going up, the glass and steel construction that teased the city with the promise of lofts and hipsters, flying by the two old brown buildings that marked a dip in the road that made our stomachs fall whenever we drove by in my parents' car, but somehow not on the bus. The route went along Lake Ontario, where I always searched eagerly for crashing waves. There were rarely any, this being a lake and not an ocean, but on cold and windy days the water could get pretty choppy.

The bus exited the Expressway on to Spadina Avenue, and headed in the direction of the Sky Dome. One year, all the Muslim communities in Toronto pooled their resources to rent it out and celebrate Eid. That's the only time I've been to the Sky Dome. As always, the organisers figured out a way to separate the men and women, even in such an enormous stadium. I stood near the entrance with my family, handing out flyers protesting the arrest and subsequent mistreatment of Shaykh Omar Abdur-Rahman – 'the Blind Sheikh', as he was called in the media. We were told he was being tortured in prison, and, specifically, that he had been raped with a broom. We were shocked at how apathetic Muslims were; many wouldn't even take the pamphlets we were distributing, brushing right past our outstretched hands as if we weren't there at all. The bus rolled past the Sky Dome, where the Blue Jays also played, and eventually pulled into the St George Campus, letting us out at the circle – we had a circle rather than a quad – right in front of the medical sciences building.

The entire trip from home to campus and back was cocooned, sheltered, safe. My dad drove me to the bus stop every morning and then picked me up from the same place when I returned in the evenings. That way, I avoided all public transportation. This was as much about safety as it was about control. Public transportation is terribly frightening if you're not used to taking it, if you're not exposed to it, and if you look different. Extremisms abound in all forms in the public space, including racist and Islamophobic ones.

I loved my time at the University of Toronto. I delighted in the buzz of the place, the grand stone buildings, the chapels, the arches, the well-worn wooden bannisters, the cosy and numerous libraries. Victoria Park, in the centre of campus, was magical on winter nights, blanketed in soft, pillowy snow that fell gently, illuminated in the glow of the globe lamps. I loved the vines that climbed the walls of New College, the green turning into the most vibrant reds and yellows and oranges in the fall. I loved the little adolescent maple tree in front of Sidney Smith that in the October sun burned a red so bright it looked like it might catch fire. It made me feel like Moses approaching the burning bush. I loved the tiny carrels in Robarts Library. In the six years I was there – four for undergrad and two for my master's – I rarely left campus to walk on Bloor Street or Yonge Street, or anywhere else. I would only discover Toronto years later, with Rumee, after first telling him there was nothing to do downtown.

I want to linger on this point. I took a bus downtown almost every day for six years and never discovered the city beyond the university campus. I explored the campus itself, had wonderful extended conversations about the meaning of life and religion with Menka, and Sarah, and Jacob, and James. I knew almost every tree on that campus, but I never left the university grounds. Why? Simply put, I never considered it. It never really occurred to me to do so, and if anyone asked to leave campus with me, I acted like I didn't want to. But it wasn't that. Or rather, maybe it was, but I interpreted my fear of leaving campus as not wanting to leave. What was I afraid of? I was afraid of being in the real world, unprotected, with my niqab. On campus, I was still

sheltered. If someone was bigoted or racist, I could technically report them, though of course I never reported anyone.
But at least there was a mechanism in place. Off campus, I
was vulnerable, exposed, without a safety net. Who would I
complain to there? Who would care? So, for all my talk
about the niqab not limiting my options, in the end, it did.

Some things were just more difficult with the niqab, like
eating most foods. You could eat small dry foods easily, like
nuts. But messy foods, even chips, if they touched the inside
of the niqab, would leave a residue, a smell, a stain that
would touch your face for the rest of the day. Drinking was
cumbersome too. It's not easy, though doable, to stick a cup
of coffee under your niqab. This had health and social
consequences. I avoided eating all day while at university.
So, if I was at school from nine till six, I just wouldn't eat.
This made it easy for me to fast, not just during Ramadan,
but throughout the year. The Prophet is said to have fasted
every Monday and Thursday and on the thirteenth, four-
teenth and fifteenth of every month in the Islamic calendar.
And during the first ten days of Dhul Hijja. And those first
days in Shawwal. So I fasted all those fasts, too. It wasn't
much of a deviation from my normal eating patterns
anyway. My brother once said, *You shouldn't get any sawab
(merit points) for fasting because you don't like eating!*

Extremist tendencies can manifest themselves in our
eating habits. When I got to New York University for my
PhD, I was diagnosed with clinical anorexia and I had to see
a nutritionist to learn how to eat, regularly, in a balanced

way. Certainly, not eating food was a way for me to feel a
sense of control over my life. But it was also just more
convenient.

All of this meant that I never went out for meals with
friends. The logistics were too complicated. It wasn't worth
the hassle. It was also difficult, though not impossible, to
work out in niqab. I took an 'Active Healthy Living' class for
a science requirement, in which we learned to use the full
offerings of the gym. A Korean classmate partnered up with
me, and we did all the activities required of us together. I
was so grateful for her because I would have never had the
confidence to even walk into the gym without her. She was
totally unfazed by my niqab. She didn't even really acknowledge it. With her at my side, I learned to use the weight
machines, played a little squash, took a tai-chi class, all while
wearing niqab. It wasn't ideal, and though I loved working
out, I didn't take it up until I stopped wearing it. Bottom
line, it's hard to work out in niqab. It seems like an obvious
point. Still, I know because I tried.

What's interesting to me about not leaving campus to explore
downtown is that it demonstrates just how much fear can
limit our horizons, our imaginative and our experiential
horizons. I mean, the moment I got on the bus in the morning, and certainly once I got to campus, I was alone and
unsupervised. I could have watched movies in theatres

within walking distance, I could have explored the parks, I could have eaten great food, I could have even removed my niqab and walked around incognito. I could have done so much, but none of it ever occurred to me. It's not that I was resisting temptation, so much as that there were no temptations to begin with. I *believed*. Like really, truly believed – in what exactly? I'm not sure. My belief wasn't about the specifics, it was more about the broad strokes of who I wasn't and who I was. I wasn't Western, I was Muslim. Even though I now know those categories, 'Muslim' and 'Western' are meaningless – the more you try to pin them down the more elusive they get – back then, they really meant something to me. I lived in a world of black and white. There was no grey.

Doesn't this black-and-white thinking lead to extremism? a friend once asked me.

Extremism is relative, I retorted. *Besides, life is black and white. When you die, you go to Heaven or Hell. There's no in between. Muslims don't believe in Purgatory.*

Most Muslims in the Muslim Students' Association at the University of Toronto were too grey for me. I rarely attended their events. The fact that their events were not fully gender segregated troubled me. Yet, I attended a co-ed university and spent countless hours in conversation with a couple of male friends I met in class. Somehow that didn't stop me from judging Muslims for falling short on gender segregation. I did attend Friday prayers in Hart House even though there wasn't a barrier between the men and women. You still gotta pray.

One Friday at Jumuʿa, there was a reporter visiting from the *Toronto Star*. She interviewed some Muslims, including me, for a piece she was working on, while a photographer took pictures. That weekend, there was a large photo of me on the front page of the 'Life and Style' section, in a dark green jilbab with gold buttons and a black niqab. I remember my family and community members were so proud of me. I was proud of me. The white female reporter, with curly blonde hair, asked me near the end of our interview, *If you had a daughter, would you make her wear niqab?*

I knew the correct liberal answer to that question, *No, of course not! I would let her choose! I'd let her wear whatever she wanted. It would be her choice.*

I would let her choose. As if we live in vacuums and don't influence our daughters with pink hats and dolls and dresses and heels and tanning beds and Botox. As though my daughter would be born into a void where she could 'freely' choose what to do with her body, free from external pressures, free from social conditioning, free to shape her desire as she wills, free to choose between covering her face or injecting it with chemicals. If those are her choices, isn't she already trapped?

In all honesty, though, it did break my heart to think of my daughter not wearing niqab. Why wouldn't she? The reporter must have picked up on the emptiness of my answer from my tone or my eyes – she didn't have much else to go on.

Yes, but you'd advise her to wear niqab? You'd be disappointed if she didn't?

She assumed that I wanted to be a mother, that I would want a heteronormative family, that I'd have children, that one of my children would be a daughter, that I'd see my values reflected in her clothing, that I'd be disappointed if she fell short. We shared all of these assumptions. We had more in common than either of us thought.

Perhaps the most seductive siren call of extremism I have encountered is white feminism. I have found that those who practise white feminism are really good at pumping you up, making you feel like *we're all in this together*, we're fighting for *women*, and if you're a woman you're failing ALL women if you don't join in and do your part. But then, when push comes to shove, when resources are scarce, or privilege is close at hand, and you're a woman of colour, they will hold your head under water to keep themselves afloat. It took real betrayal and heartbreak for me to finally learn this lesson, that, like Islam, there are different kinds of feminism, and some are white supremacist while others are genuinely egalitarian. Just like patriarchal Islam assumes the male as its normative subject, white feminism assumes white women as its normative subject. Like patriarchal Muslims who go on about equality but support laws that discriminate against women, those who practise white feminism prattle on about equality for all, but cast their votes for white supremacists. I learned this lesson in stages and my education started early.

By the time I started my second year of university, I was in love with the place and attending full time. I was especially enjoying my Philosophy classes. I joined study groups whenever possible; they were fun and a great way to ensure a good grade. You could exchange notes, ask each other to explain an idea and rely on one another to do an extra reading or recap a missed class. In one Philosophy class, a beautiful girl named Ariana organised our study group. Ariana and I became fast friends. We started emailing each other outside of class, we'd sit next to each other, passing notes, rolling our eyes when the white male professor made yet another sexist comment. I started looking forward to Tuesday and Thursday mornings at eleven when I'd walk into the auditorium where the Philosophy class was held. Thick red velvet seat covers and red carpeting made it a cosy space despite the large classroom size. I'd look for Ariana, who'd watch for me and wave me over, usually keeping a seat free for me next to her. I felt close to her in body and spirit. We talked endlessly, but more importantly, we laughed together. We didn't agree about everything, but that was okay. In her presence, I felt seen.

Then one day, a few weeks before the end of the semester, I opened my email and saw a message from Ariana. Excitedly, I clicked on it, saw that it was kind of long, and settled in to read. But as I read, I was filled with sadness, and shame, and finally anger. Ariana wrote to say that she couldn't keep quiet any longer. She felt compelled to speak up. She didn't understand how someone as intelligent and articulate and funny as me could freely choose to live a life of subjugation and oppression while living in a country like Canada, where I could be free, and where no one would persecute me for being independent and liberated. She was hoping that all the hours and weeks she spent getting to know me would give her some insight, help her understand, or help her turn me, unveil me, so to speak, but it had only made her angry and confused. She hated that I chose to wear niqab and that I insisted that I wasn't oppressed – this offended her. How could I see myself as free when clearly I was caged, erased, faceless, serving a patriarchal religion? So, even as she promised me that I lived in a country where I wouldn't be persecuted for expressing my independence by wearing whatever I wanted, she found my choices intolerable. And she just had to tell me all this because she respected me and cared about me. Classic abusive words. *I'm hurting you because I love you.*

I read her email with ringing ears, wind sweeping my mind, which was suddenly a desert, with brown balls of tumbleweed flying about, flimsy, unmoored and directionless. My mouth ran dry. My heart broke again and again as I read and reread Ariana's message. In disbelief. In pain.

This whole time I'd thought we were friends, but in fact, she had been trying to figure out if I was fully human. All she saw was a shadow of me, a flat two-dimensional image, a representation of ideas rather than a delightful, complex, full person. Which is to say, she didn't see me at all. And she saw herself as apart from, as different, as special, as free, because she wore different clothes than me. She thought that she could see, but that I was blind; like she had clarity and perspective while I was chained to ignorance. She wanted to save a person who was not looking to be saved. And that pissed her off.

Beware the one who seeks to save you on the assumption of her own exceptionalism.

Ariana couldn't see me as a full human, as someone who might relate to the world differently than she did, who might make different choices. This angered me; what difference did it make to her what I wore? Why did my clothing choice affect our relationship so profoundly and fundamentally? How dare she decide what I needed to wear in order to be 'free'? What kind of feminism was this?

White feminism.

In his allegory of the cave, Plato describes a people who live shackled in a cave and see the world only through shadows cast on the walls. They mistake these shadows for the real world. But there are some people, some exceptional people, who break their shackles, leave the cave and see the world beyond the shadows, as it truly is, and thus they are able to see the shadows for what they truly are. These special people try to tell the cave-dwellers about the world beyond the cave, they want to free them from their shackles by telling them about a world bathed in light. But the cave-dwellers are at once restricted by and invested in the shadows, because that is the only world they know, the world they see, the world they understand, the world they can imagine. A universe beyond the shadows is unbelievable to them, it is frightening, it is threatening. And though it seems impossible that anything might exist beyond the shadows, an entire colourful, textured universe awaits them, if only they would permit themselves to step outside, traverse a few yards and just *see*, let their eyes be open and behold. Once they see the world, it will become clear to them that they've been living in shadows their entire lives. And the shadows will never be enough again.

I loved this allegory when I first learned it in my university Philosophy classes, when extremism was still appealing to me. But now I get its destructive power, how it justifies the elevation of some over others by gliding over some really important questions. Like, why are there people shackled in the cave? Who put them there? Who are these special people who have escaped? How have they escaped? What makes them so special? And who has the power to 'unshackle' the shackled? What is the price of the unshackling? The allegory of the cave cultivates a class of special, saved, exceptional people, people who are better than everyone else and thus in a position to save others, even when they might not want to be saved. When you read more about Plato, you realise this was exactly his intention.

Beware the one who seeks to save you on the assumption of their own exceptionalism.

The very idea of some people being exceptional, being saved, being special, is delusional, because it requires everyone else to be unexceptional, unspecial, even shackled. Toni Morrison once said, *If you can only be tall because someone else is on their knees, then you have a serious problem.* This principle holds true for any kind of exceptionalism; if you need people to be shackled so you can feel free, then you're not free. You're just an extremist.

The FBI, Queen Victoria, Israr Ahmed, the colonialists, John Doe, Ariana, and me too, we were all participating in extremist discourses, presuming ourselves exceptional, as the ones able to see the truth of the world as it was, as bringing the light to those in shadows, to those we imagined shackled in a cave, content in their own ignorance. But we were the ignorant ones, the ones with narrow imaginations, the ones who could not see, the ones who hurt others while claiming to help them. The principles and beliefs of extremists, their positions even, can vary wildly, but they come to them in the same exclusionary, intolerant way, confident in their own superiority and exceptionalism, certain that they are privy to knowledge no one else has, that they are uniquely positioned to rectify others, show them the way, save them.

You don't have to adhere to a formal religion to be a zealot. Extremism comes in many forms. In all of its forms, it is shallow and cruel.

Jet Skiing on the Mediterranean

The first summer that I was in Syria, I spent most of my time in Damascus, where I befriended a South Asian woman, who, like me, was in her early twenties. She came from a wealthy family in the United States. She was worldly and cool. She got me to consider bending the rules of my highly disciplined and meticulously organised life. We'd stay up late, talking into the night, we'd smoke sheesha, miss Fajr and skip classes at the University of Damascus to explore the Old City. She got me to see young Muslim couples holding hands, being affectionate with each other, as adorable rather than disgusting. She taught me that public displays of affection were cute, sweet even. We spent that summer acting like death was impossible and like we had all the time in the world. Which is to say, we were reckless.

At one point, we decided to visit the Mediterranean so that we could say we went. We got on a bus from Damascus to the coastal town of Latakia. We arrived in the dead of night. When we got off the bus, some guy offered us a ride to our hotel, and we readily accepted, seeing this as a generosity. At one point, he turned on to a mud road that wound through a field. It was dark and we couldn't see the road ahead of us, we didn't know exactly where we were going; we were filled with fear and thrill, as we realised just how dangerous this situation was. No one knew where we were. Anything could happen. Thankfully, the man was upstanding and delivered us to our hotel.

The next afternoon, on a bright sunny day, we frolicked in the water, me wearing tights, a T-shirt, a jilbab and niqab. Of course, no one there knew me or would care if I didn't wear a jilbab or niqab, but it didn't occur to me to wear anything different. I was more comfortable in it than without it.

In the distance, we saw people on jet skis.

C'mon! Let's jet ski! my friend said. She had ridden jet skis before, but I hadn't. *It'll be fun!*

In the back of my mind, I knew that all of these experiences – the late-night trip to a seaside town, the playing on the beach, the jet skiing – would be useful back in Canada. One of the ways that I managed people's emotions about my niqab was to trick them away from their fear, or shock, or disgust and engage them in lively conversation, tell them something they didn't expect to hear, like that I had gone jet skiing on the Mediterranean. I brought this up as evidence of the complexity of niqabi women, of my own complexity. In other words, I brought it up as evidence of my humanity.

See? You don't know anything about the experience of niqabi women! When you see a niqabi, you just see the fabric, not the woman wearing it!

When I was younger, I used to think that this was a brilliant move. Now I realise that Islamophobic ideas are so entrenched that even people who make their living off of examining complex ideas have trouble seeing niqabi women as complex humans.

Recently, I shared an essay from this book, 'Assimilation', with a group of mostly white academics at a prestigious university in the United States. The essay was written to highlight the many overlapping reasons why Muslim women may or may not cover. In the Q&A, a white woman said that it infuriated her, made her angry, that *they made their women cover so much over there*. In her comment, 'they' and 'over there' could have referred to Pakistanis and Pakistan, or Muslims and anywhere Muslims exist.

The 'they' and the 'over there' were figments of her imagination, rather than any real people or places on Earth. Yet her imagination and her sentiments dominated the discussion for the next hour. Even though the central point of my essay is that racism led my parents to embrace fundamentalist Islam in Canada, somehow the discussion devolved into the problem with Islam and Muslims, rather than racism and liberal intolerance. I fielded question after question about Pakistani culture and Islam; I watched my esteemed colleagues indulge in righteous rage against a religion that might oppress Pakistani Muslim women, even as they steadily ignored the danger posed to those very same Pakistani Muslim women by drone warfare waged by the country in which we were all present. In their self-righteous imagination, veils were more outrageous than bombs.

Not long ago, I was at a mostly white party in Canada, where a white gay man living in India – where he ran a business and made his livelihood off of Indians – in the first thirty seconds of meeting me, uttered this sentence: *When I see women in niqab, I just want to rip it off their faces!*

He made a snatching motion with his hand when he said 'rip'. The fact that he said 'rip', a word that denotes violence, indicates he did not give a fuck about the women in niqab. He was moved to violence and felt justified about it. Virtuous even. Brazen.

That level of dehumanisation is widespread; you hear it in the righteous indignation of liberal elites in Western nations under the guise of gender equality, and you hear it from conservative governments and clerics who compel women to cover under the guise of morality. You hear it in official decrees, and in academic venues, and in casual discourse, where women in burqas are referred to as 'walking tents'. It's not the burqa dehumanising those women, it is the people who see a walking tent where a woman walks.

This reductive way of thinking, measuring liberation or oppression through the length of fabric, erases the women wearing the cloth. They are two sides of the same coin; the people who are so obsessed with the veil that they'll force women to wear it and those who cannot abide the women who do; neither is interested in the humanity of the women doing the covering or uncovering.

Get over yourselves! I sometimes want to scream at these people. *You are not the most important person in this conversation. Maybe try listening instead of speaking first.*

So, to get people to listen, one of the things I repeated, over and over again, as I sought to shatter stereotypes of niqabi women, was that I'd travelled by myself to the Middle East, that I'd climbed Mount Sinai in the middle of the night to watch sunrise, that I'd jet skied on the Mediterranean, all while wearing niqab.

The niqab doesn't stop me from anything! I would say.

Somehow, I thought that listing these activities, holding them out as proofs, as evidence of my humanity, would help people see that I was human – a person who did things, beheld beauty, enjoyed life. But it was a degrading and dehumanising enterprise, with me saying, *Lookit what I did, I'm human!* And them saying, in the best-case scenario, *Wow, I had no idea you were human!*

What did these conversations cost me, the human always trying to prove her humanity? It cost me the ability to process the experience of being in my body, to be honest about what happened to my body, how I really felt about it. The politicised nature of the veil made me feel that I couldn't speak about my actual experiences with any depth or complexity, without worrying about how it would look to others. Would my experiences, my stories, confirm or challenge what people thought about Muslims, or the veil? Would my experiences be generalised as 'Muslim' or 'South Asian'? I knew my experiences would never be generalised as 'Canadian', so how would they be generalised?

There is little room for honesty, for truth, in this space. And if there was a chance that my experiences might confirm the worst suspicions of racists and misogynists and Islamophobes, then memories, events, experiences, happenings, truths – they got forgotten, suppressed, erased, disappeared. As if they hadn't happened. As if the whole of my life experience was simple, uncomplicated. As simple and uncomplicated as the boxes people wanted to put me in, the person they expected, even needed me to be. But really, the person I wasn't and could never be. Because there is no simple, uncomplicated person. No one fits in a box. Ever. Humans, by their very definition, are leaky. We cannot be contained.

There was no official place to rent jet skis, so my friend and I approached a couple of guys who had a jet ski of their own and asked if they'd rent it out to us. After some negotiation, we agreed on a price. But one of the guys insisted that my friend and I couldn't go out together on our own, that he'd have to take each of us separately. You know, for safety. One of us would sit up front and 'drive' while he sat behind us, making sure we didn't get hurt. In case you're wondering, no, we didn't have life vests, and no, I did not know how to swim.

My friend went first. I waited on the shore with the other guy. We watched silently as the two of them sped off into the distance, getting tinier and tinier and then larger and larger as they returned. Then it was my turn. The afternoon was turning to evening by now, the sun beginning to descend behind the mountains in the distance. It was getting cloudier and colder. I suddenly was no longer crazy about going out on a jet ski and getting wet again. And yet, when the young man gestured me forward, I got on. I didn't know yet that I could just change my mind. That I was entitled to do so. That I could do the opposite of what I'd just said because now I felt differently. That feeling differently was a good enough reason to not go through with a plan. I got on that jet ski for all the haters out there, so I could say I'd done yet another thing as a niqabi.

As we set out, the guy showed me how to steer, how to turn the throttle to speed up. Once I got the hang of it, it was thrilling. The speed at which you could move, the danger, the flirting with death. At some level, I knew this was insanely reckless behaviour. Again, I didn't know how to swim.

My jilbab was hiked up around my waist so I could straddle the jet ski, and my legs, clad in black tights, were exposed.

At some point, while I was caught up in the fun, the fear, the excitement of the jet ski, I felt hands on my thighs. I looked down and saw the guy's hands. The nail of the pinky finger of his right hand was very long. And the hands were moving. They started caressing my inner thighs and moved up into my crotch. I was stunned. I couldn't speak. I couldn't say, *Stop! Stop doing that!*

I was at this guy's mercy, on the fucking Mediterranean, on a jet ski, without a life vest, unable to swim. I knew, in my core, that the balance of power was in his favour. He could do what he damn well pleased. Joy and thrill curdled into sickening shame in the pit of my stomach. I felt dirty. And damaged. And sick. And dirty. Like *I* was doing something wrong. I hated myself there, on that jet ski. I hated myself for being so stupid as to find myself in this situation, for being so cowardly as to not speak up, to not say *no, stop!*, for not slapping his hands away.

Eventually, we turned around. As we got closer to shore, he pulled his hands away. I jumped off quickly, avoiding eye contact. Though I remember his hands clearly, I do not remember his face. I wouldn't recognise him if I saw him today. That is, if Assad's bombings have not killed him, if he hasn't drowned in the Mediterranean trying to escape the hell that Syria has become. He might be in a refugee camp in Turkey, or he might have joined ISIS. If he is still alive, that is.

My friend and I walked back quietly. The mood turned from light-hearted and adventurous to heavy silence. It was dark enough by now that we couldn't see each other's faces.

Did that guy touch you on the jet ski? my friend asked.

No!

The word was out of my mouth before I could catch it. I lied to cover my shame. As if the lie were a garment, and a garment might actually cover my shame. Like Adam and Eve, I figured, if I could just cover myself with something, even something flimsy, like a lie, like a leaf, it would be enough.

He felt up my breasts, she confessed.

Then why did you let me get on the jet ski with him?! I wanted to scream.

And also this: I was shocked by her confession. I couldn't believe that she would admit to such a thing, say it out loud, like it didn't taint her, like she carried no blame. Her lack of shame stunned me. *I* was ashamed. So ashamed, I lied to a friend. So ashamed, the shame spilled out of me and enveloped her. Rather than confess to the groping I too experienced, I left her stranded, alone, isolated. I offered her no solace, just silence. What I offered myself might have been worse: denial.

At least she had spoken her truth, out loud, without shame. Even if she spoke it too late to save me.

The ones we love are keepers of our shame. They can reinforce it or they can help untangle us from it, help us be free of it. Shame is nurtured in community, it gathers its strength in hushed tones, in whispers and secrets, until it becomes so loud as to be deafening. Shame wants to spread. Others must buy into it or it dissipates. Like the fog that can be so thick as to blot out entire mountains, that can press down, close in and feel suffocating, feel eternal; fog that resists mightily the light of the sun, standing its ground, retreating a bit and then returning with vigour. But that same fog can evaporate under the light and disappear so completely as to leave no trace of itself, barely even a memory.

I suppressed what happened out there on the Mediterranean. Silenced it, wrapped it up in fog, because there was no place for it. This wasn't supposed to happen to niqabi women – that's what I'd been told my whole life.

The hijab protects you! Even more so the niqab!

By the time I returned to Canada at the end of that summer, I was trotting out the line about jet skiing on the Mediterranean in niqab as yet another item that proved my humanity. *That's just how badass she is,* I wanted others to think. I unremembered what happened to me out there, on the Mediterranean. I lived in fog.

More than a decade later, when the fog lifted and I re-remembered, my heart broke for my friend, and also for that young niqabi girl. I feel compassion for her naïveté. She didn't understand yet that the horror and the sorrow of patriarchy is that all of its truths are lies. That none of the things it tells us will save us can save us. And worse still, when we learn that the lies of patriarchy are what they are

– lies – we are forced to cover for it, manufacture shame, blame ourselves for the failures of patriarchy, lie to ourselves and others to protect patriarchy. But the shame and the lies, they are fog, they obscure the truth, prevent us from seeing what lies before us.

Now I know better. I know that patriarchy hates women and that it nurtures shame in us to compensate for its own failures, that shame makes lying necessary. I know now that shame hurts everything it touches. Shame makes it difficult to have compassion, to help a friend in need, to accept help. Makes it difficult to come together, to care for one another, to love each other. Love is the light that takes away the fog of shame.

The fact is, there is no cool story that will get people to see me as human if all they see is a 'walking tent'. Just like no amount of clothing can keep me from being assaulted when people see a sexual object where a human stands. To see a human where one sees a 'walking tent', you have to be able to love the person before you, on her own terms. To see the humanity of someone who decides not to cover in the way you think best, you have to love her. Again, on her own terms.

But to love others on their own terms, we must first love ourselves. I see now that I've always misunderstood the commandment to love one's neighbour as oneself. I thought it meant we were supposed to love for our neighbours what we loved for ourselves. But that's just another way of universalising our desires and imposing them on others. There's nothing noble or loving about that. Instead of assuming that we love ourselves already and challenging us to love others in the same way, the commandment asks us to love ourselves fully, even – especially – the parts of ourselves we'd rather not look at, the parts we are ashamed of, so that we can love others fully, too. Loving like this is hard. It takes practice, it is best cultivated in community. We cannot offer others love, kindness, compassion that we do not first feel for ourselves.

After all, فاقد الشيئ لا يعطيه

The one who does not have something cannot give it.

Hair Diaries

I spent a few years as a fellow at two Institutes for Advanced Study, and in that time, I've had many sustained conversations with mathematicians. Mathematicians, I have found, like to talk about beauty in an abstract, non-political way. Beauty as symmetry, beauty as patterns, repetitions and rhythms, rather than beauty as socially constructed, as subjective, as gendered, as racial. Many of the ones I have been in conversation with cannot even imagine the political, the contested, the subjective, the weaponised nature of beauty. And if they can, they don't see it as relevant to their discussions of beauty. They see themselves as adherents of a different religion – one that reveres a purer, higher, cleaner form of beauty, beauty untainted by human subjectivity. Objective beauty. Beauty that is at once free of human frailty yet somehow recognisable to the human eye, independent of human bias and yet somehow captured by the human mind. They can't see that there is no such thing, that there can be no beauty detached from human complexity and variety and subjectivity. Once human senses, the mind, is involved, nothing is objective. It is all argument. It is all contested. It is all political.

'Aesthetic' is a relative to 'beauty'. As in, *Oh, I love this aesthetic!* or, *This aesthetic doesn't speak to me.* Aesthetic is subjective too, like beauty. It is gendered and racial. It creates a hierarchy, which is to say an argument for what is better and what is less than. Monotone or colourful clothing. Minimalist or ornate interiors. Small or large women. Glass or brick buildings. Black or blond hair. Pigmented or pink skin. Bald or hairy heads. Bald or hairy legs. Bald or hairy armpits. Bald or hairy faces.

Beauty is always a moral argument, because it simultaneously makes claims about what is ugly. 'Fair', as in *the fair-skinned girl* is an excellent example of a word that makes an argument for beauty that is both moral and racial. 'Fair' means pretty and beautiful. 'Fair' means light-skinned, white or whiter. 'Fair' means just, equitable, upright, trustworthy, honourable. 'Fair' does not mean ugly, it does not mean partial, biased, prejudiced, unjust. 'Fair' does not mean dark-skinned. Fair is good. The opposite of fair is bad.

Arguments about beauty are arguments about the good. Code words are used to fool us into missing the arguments that are being made about beauty, to avoid scrutiny, to escape critique. Clean is a common code word for beauty. What is clean is assumed to be beautiful and vice versa. An unclean body is ugly. A clean body is good. A dirty body is bad. You must be ashamed of a dirty body.

I have spent my life trying to be beautiful, to be clean, to be good.

1959

Some of the most bitter fights I have had with my mother were over my hair. Of course there was the drama with covering the hair on my head. When could I start covering it? When must I always cover it? Discussions about hijab are discussions about hair. Still, there's so much more to my hair than its covering. Of course there is.

According to my mother, 'good' girls always had their hair well oiled, parted down the middle in two braids. This was her dream for her daughters. She's the youngest daughter in a family of over a dozen children. Her sisters were all older, much older, maybe by a decade or so. She has vivid memories of her sisters oiling and braiding her hair, threading it with parandas, which are like extensions. Parandas are usually made of cotton, sometimes they are black or brown, to match the colour of most South Asian hair. Other times, they are bright and colourful, like the feathers of a peacock: sky blue, royal purple, hot pink, bright yellow or multicoloured. Frequently, there is some gold threaded through, or wrapped around the ends. A paranda comes joined at the head with three strands, you can weave it into your own braid, to make the hair look longer, thicker, more colourful, more beautiful. If your hair is too short, a paranda will fall out after a few hours.

When she was an itty-bitty girl, my mother loved having parandas braided through her hair, which, at the time, was short and thick. She especially wanted, demanded them when she went to school. It made her feel like an adult, and special, to have a paranda hanging down her back, bouncing against her bum. But the problem was that her hair was short and thick, so the paranda was likely to slip out before she returned home from school. Her older sisters, who oiled and braided her hair, thought that parandas were superfluous, wasted even, on my mother, because she was bound to lose them. But my mother wouldn't have any of it. She told us, with sparkling eyes and an easy laugh, lost in the memory of this happy time, that she'd throw a fit when her sisters refused to braid her hair with a paranda. She'd throw a tantrum so her father would hear her, and then he'd take her side, chiding her sisters for not giving her what she wanted.

What's it to you? he'd scold them. *Just braid her hair with a paranda!*

But Abba-ji, parandas are not free, and she's just going to lose it!

You're not paying for it, I am! he'd retort.

And her sisters would fume, they'd be seething as they pulled her hair unnecessarily hard, yanked her head while twisting her braid. They'd weave in a paranda and threaten to beat her with scissors if she came home without it.

And sure enough, every afternoon, my mother returned home with her hair in disarray, the paranda nowhere to be found.

1985

These memories of childhood hair braiding were formative for my mother, because despite all the drama-bazi, the yanked hair, the case for and against the paranda, the screaming, the confrontation between her father and her sisters, these times spent braiding hair were moments of closeness, care, love between sisters. They were sites of intimacy. My khalas would touch my mother, caress her hair as they oiled it, parted it in the middle, braided it. She'd be sitting at their feet, between their legs, they'd be on a chaarpai maybe, or a piri. My mother wanted to recreate these loving, intimate moments with her daughters. I'm sure she'd imagined it many times, since she didn't have a younger sister herself to boss around, whose hair she could oil and braid, whom she could chide and forgive for losing a paranda. Now she had daughters of her own. Who'd stand in her way?

I would! I didn't want my hair oiled at all. The oil smelled strong, which I interpreted as 'bad', it looked oily. In Pakistan, shiny, braided hair might be beautiful, but in Canada, oily, braided hair isn't exactly high fashion. I didn't want my hair parted down the middle, I wanted it parted off to the side, a little askew, like a hat at a jaunty angle. And I certainly didn't want my hair braided; I wanted to let it hang loose, flowing, so I could flick it back over my shoulder, maybe as I laughed, maybe as I stood around with a group of friends, maybe as I delivered a well-timed joke. I wanted to be like the girls at school, who were mostly white, none of whom had oiled or braided hair. I knew that oily, tightly braided hair was 'old-fashioned' and 'fob-y' at school, 'dirty' even, but at home, loose-flowing hair was 'modern' and 'Western'. Women with loose hair might be loose in other ways, too.

As always, there were pragmatic reasons for my mother's strict rules around hair. It is difficult to wear loose hair under a hijab and under a dupatta. It makes the dupatta slip off easily, and with a hijab, well, it's just a mess. It becomes jumbled, it wraps around your neck, strands inevitably begin to poke out, insisting on being seen even as you keep pushing them back under the hijab. Besides, with four South Asian, Punjabi daughters with hair as thick as ours, I'm sure that braids helped with cleanliness. In my carpet-less apartment, I'm acutely aware of just how much hair I shed on a daily basis. Imagine my hair multiplied by five – that's a lot of hair to clean up. Recently, I went to buy a Dyson vacuum cleaner, and the salesman recommended the model designed to pick up animal hair. When I said that I don't have any pets, he nodded toward my head.

Are you calling me an animal? I asked indignantly.

No! But you do have a lot of hair! he protested, his face flushed red.

My mother mostly got her way with my hair while I lived at home, right through grade school and high school. By the time I was in university, my mother was getting softer on the issue; now, when she occasionally oiled and braided my hair,

I appreciated it for the loving and intimate act it had become. I have nostalgic memories of sitting at my mother's feet as she pours oil into the middle of my scalp, as I feel it trickle down my head, as she rubs it in with the base of her palm, a wonderfully relaxing head massage thrown in as part of the package. She massages my temples and my neck too, sometimes hitting my head gently, with quick strikes from the side of her hand, poised as if to deliver a karate chop. It feels so deeply comforting to be tended to in this way, tenderly, to be at her mercy like this, to be her child.

But when I was younger, especially in grade school, I saw the oiling and the braiding of my hair as a unique act of oppression and tyranny. I hated the funky smell of the oils my mother used, Johnson & Johnson baby oil mixed with sticky mustard oil, or olive oil, and sometimes pungent green Amla oil. I'd be at her feet, she'd sit on a chair or on the edge of the bathtub or a bed. Fat tears would roll down my face. I'd weep as my mother oiled and braided my hair. When I looked at myself in the mirror after my mother had finished, I only ever saw ugliness.

And on top of these hair wars, there was the covering of hair, with a hijab when I was out, and with a dupatta or chador when I was at home.

بال ڈھکو! *Cover your hair!* – an oft-repeated command.

بال نظر آ رہے ہیں! *Your hair is showing!* – a common rebuke.

2004

It probably comes as no surprise that my mother cut our hair herself. We never went to a salon. When you have six children, salons are expensive, even the lower-end ones. That means that my mother and I fought over the length of my hair, too. Sometimes my mother cut my hair too short when I wanted it longer, other times she barely trimmed it when I wanted it shorter. A few times, when I was in grade school, she got so sick and overwhelmed by my hair, she just sheared it all off. Without any prior warning. That was a new kind of nakedness, being shorn like that, unexpectedly, like a lamb. I was relieved I wore a hijab back then, because at least I didn't have to suffer public ridicule on top of this violation.

I was disappointed by every single haircut my mother gave me, mostly because I wanted to be beautiful. And beautiful, in my head, was Anne of Green Gables. So the only haircut that could have pleased me was one that replaced me with a freckled, white-skinned, red-haired girl, turning me into someone I was not, erasing me. My poor mother didn't stand a chance.

I started visiting hair salons once I was living on my own. At first I searched for salons with female stylists who agreed to cut my hair after hours, when the salon was closed, ensuring that no man would accidentally walk in and see me without my hijab. When that became a nuisance, I started getting my hair cut during normal hours, regardless of male presence. I'd arrive at the salon with my hair covered, get my hair cut and then leave with my hijab back on my head, ruining the blow-out. Once I stopped wearing hijab, a few of my stylists were male. That felt really scandalous and I had to breathe my way through those haircuts, reminding myself that I wasn't doing anything wrong.

In my thirties, I came to love my brown skin and black hair. I love my hair's thickness, its lusciousness. But first, I tried to destroy it. For a few years, I highlighted it with blond streaks. My passport picture, taken long ago, captures the damage I did in those years. When border agents look at the picture, they glance back at me, then back down at the picture, then back at me. If they are people of colour, I joke, apologetically, *I thought I was white back then.* They laugh knowingly.

Now that I'm more comfortable in my South Asian body, I only colour my hair to its original colour – black #3. I'm not yet fully comfortable in my human body, or with time, or with mortality, so I'm not ready to accept my white hair. Hair dye has ammonia in it, which is a toxic chemical. You know something is dangerous when the people advocating it start playing semantic games.

Is ammonia harmful? I ask.

'Harmful' is a tricky word, they reply.

My stylists warn me that non-ammonia hair dye is less effective.

But isn't ammonia dangerous? I ask them, hoping they'll say, *No, not at all!*

Instead they say, *Yeah, girl! But you pee it right out!*

Another says, *No pain, no gain, right?* as she slathers the dye into my hair, my scalp, my body. My body absorbs this toxicity, so that I might be beautiful. And I bury my head in the sand and wish and wish and wish away all side effects, all cancer, all possible negative results from the mutilations I put my body through, this good and beautiful body . . . for who? For beauty. Beauty for whom?

I hate it when stylists say, *Whoa! You have A LOT of hair!* like it's a judgement, or a challenge, or an abnormality. Or when they say, *You have THICK hair!*

I've finally started saying, *A lot of hair compared to who? Thick hair compared to who?* Because my hair is not thick for South Asian hair, it's normal for South Asian hair.

When I first started going to salons, the white stylists would thin out my hair, because they thought it was a problem that I had so much of it. Now, I look for hair stylists who are themselves people of colour. They don't comment on the volume of my hair, except to appreciate it, and they have never tried to thin it out.

You have such beautiful hair! they tell me, as they run their fingers through it, lovingly.

It's nice when we get cues from others that help us accept, even love ourselves – when others make us feel beautiful, good – rather than cues that make us hate ourselves, afraid of ourselves, like there is something abnormal, wrong, ugly about us. Cues that encourage us to embrace, celebrate, reveal ourselves, rather than police, suppress and erase ourselves.

1999

As a Punjabi woman, I have far more hair on my body than just the hair on my head. My people have a lot of hair. Many of us think we have too much hair. ALL of this hair has been the subject of too much attention, too much discussion, scrutiny and worry. When I hit puberty, my hair came in thick and strong. It was everywhere. Coiled and coarse, my pubic hair held on to pungent odours. My armpits filled with dense hair that smelled strongly and became slippery from sweat. My arms and legs and hands and toes were covered with long, thick hair. And then there was the hair on my face, on my upper lip, on my cheeks, on my chin. It felt like an abomination, a curse, a scourge.

The hair on our head was attractive, beautiful, good but needed to be controlled and covered as much as possible. All the other hair on my body was unattractive, ugly, bad and needed to be either removed entirely or trimmed. There was a fundamental contradiction here. On the one hand, we covered our heads, our faces, our bodies, even our hands – with pretty silk ballgown gloves purchased from the Bay, to protect ourselves from the desirous male gaze. Men were expected to have an uncontrollable desire for the female body. Ontologically. Which means, that's just how they were made, in their essence. Which means they had no control over their desire, over themselves. Which means they couldn't possibly be held accountable for their behaviour when overcome by desire.

I remember one religious preacher, a dentist by training and a cleric by presumption, describing male sexual desire as ravenous, untamed. He said, *Men are like wolves. Asking men to control their sexual desire is like asking us not to be men. Men are sexual wolves. Predatory. Aggressive. That's how God made us, we can't help it. Sometimes we feel hungry. Sometimes we feel thirsty. Sometimes we feel sexy.*

On the other hand, even as we wore clothing to thwart the male gaze, an abstract and desirous male gaze filtered into our most private, intimate lives, defined our relationship to our bodies, dictated our relationship to our hair, to ourselves. Our grooming practices, even those in areas men would never see, catered to the male gaze. The mythic male gaze, because in this strictly segregated heteronormative world, no male actually told me which hair to keep and which to remove, what was attractive and what wasn't. We just knew we had to be desirable, both in terms of our bodies and our character. As for our character, any strength that approached independence and resistance was meant to be reformulated, reshaped into strength that was patient, yielding, long-suffering. And as for our bodies, hair had to be changed, altered, controlled.

Hair on our head was beautiful. Long hair was best, we couldn't cut our hair short. That was too modern. Too Western, too unfeminine; which is to say, too masculine. What is normal, even attractive on men, became unappealing, unsightly, ugly on women.

As for the hair that grew naturally on the rest of our bodies, suddenly that became 'unnatural'. This hair had to be removed, trimmed, controlled. The Prophet said, as related to me by my mother, pubic hair and armpit hair was to be trimmed to no longer than one-third of your finger. It's possible that this demand to trim pubic and armpit hair had hygienic roots. But hygiene has always been connected to ideas about purity and virtue. These grooming prescriptions might also have emerged from a place of deep loathing for the human body, so that it must be transformed, 'cleaned', in order to be desirable, in order to be holy. In this vision, the prepubescent body is the ideal body type, and the healthy, natural growth of hair on an adult female body must be removed for it to be clean and desirable. A female body with all its hair intact is shameful, undesirable and unclean. There is a close connection between cleanliness and shame. The Prophet said:

Haya [shame] is a branch of iman [faith].

And also that, صفائ آدھا ایمان ہے *Cleanliness is half of faith.*

So basically, if you have shame and are clean, you're more than halfway home.

1993

The onset of puberty heralded an endless obsession with hair removal. We started out with waxing. First at the hands of expert women, whom we paid to remove our hair. My mother never spent her hard-earned and carefully counted money getting our hair cut, but she spent it to have our hair removed from our bodies. We got our hair removed by South Asian and Arab immigrants, women who ran beauty parlours out of their living rooms and dens. They charged $20 to wax your face.

They'd boil down sugar until it turned into a beautiful golden wax with plenty of elasticity. This made it possible for them to apply a thick coat of it on to your skin while still hot – not so hot as to burn your skin but hot enough to spread evenly on to your legs, or arms, or armpits, or face. This part was pleasant. It felt nice. Then they'd take a strip of cloth and place it on top of the wax, using their hands to rub the strips into the skin, making sure it adhered. This, too, felt nice, almost loving. Next, they'd grab the strip from one end and rip it off your skin, pulling the thick black hair out. If it was a clean swipe, if the wax had been boiled to the correct consistency, and if the cotton strip had adhered strongly to the wax, then the hair would be pulled out by the roots, lying mostly flat against the golden wax except for the roots themselves, which curled gently upward. Rows upon rows of perfectly round white heads looking up at you.

However, if the wax was poorly made, under- or over-cooked, the hair would enjoy a momentary victory. The wax might peel your skin off along with the hair, or tug at your hair but not hard enough to pull it out by its roots. There would be a whole lot of pain for no reward, just a mess. Hair coated in sugary, syrupy goop, sore follicles. Then you'd try again. Even when it worked perfectly, in those teenage years, the follicles would often bleed, because the roots were thick and strong. You'd be left with red, stinging skin and tiny droplets of blood where hair grew just seconds before. The hair did not want to be pulled out. It punished you for removing it.

I remember my mother taking me to an Iraqi woman's place to remove the hair from my armpit. The woman lived in a condo in Mississauga. She wore a jilbab in her own home. Not out of modesty; it's easier to wear a jilbab at home when guests or clients visit. It takes the pressure off what you're wearing, of thinking about wearing the right outfit. This woman had small children, at least two, watching us with their big brown eyes and curly blond hair. One was on her hip, the other was by the door. When the woman saw my armpit hair, thick and long and dense, she recoiled. Like she had seen something hideous. That's the first time I realised that my normal, natural body might be repulsive to others.

My skin would turn red and it would sting from the waxing but soon after it felt soft and tender and clean. When it was freshly waxed, my skin got very hot. I guess all the blood rushed to the surface, from the trauma of waxing. I liked it. I caressed it. It felt good. Desirable.

To whom?

To the abstract male gaze. To the man who might love me. And touch me. And not be repulsed by me.

The man I married was really a boy because we were both twenty-three years old. Children, really, when I think back on it. Neither he nor I had been with anyone else, and he was surprised to learn that I did not have hair on my legs. His mom had told him that Muslim girls didn't shave; waxing wasn't even something he could conceive of, and he was shocked, but excited, that I waxed my legs for him. I realise now that he might have loved the hair on my legs, if I'd had any, because he loved everything about me, just as I was. He didn't know yet, precisely, the cost – physical, financial, emotional, psychological – of hair removal. The lengths to which I was willing to go for it. How much I had to hate my body to suffer so deeply to alter it, to make it beautiful. To make it clean. To make it good.

2007

Hair removal has been a central fixture in my life. When Rumee and I visited Yemen together, alongside studying legal texts and reading manuscripts in archives, I found time to get waxed. We were graduate students at the time, without much money. Our big weekly splurge was a $30 buffet brunch that was offered between eleven o'clock and three o'clock each Sunday at the Mövenpick Hotel. We would show up at 10:55A.M. with a bunch of other graduate students, place a timer in the centre of the table and fill our bellies at a steady pace for four hours. Every few weeks, I would follow up brunch with a trip to the hotel spa, where I would spend $50 to get my body waxed – my face, my arms, my legs, my armpits.

I never summoned the courage for a Brazilian wax, though I considered it from time to time. I used to shave and now I trim my hair down there, as per my mother's Islamic prescriptions. It's funny, when you think about it, which aspects of religion stay with you, and which are easily shed.

Valuable and scarce financial resources were often channelled toward the removal of unwanted hair. My dear mother taught kids Qur'an recitation five days a week, for two hours per day. She charged her students $20 per week. That's $5 per day, $2.50 per hour. Fridays were free. And she used some of this money to take me to a laser hair removal studio, paying $150 every six weeks to remove hair from my face, to erase the moustache and beard that grew strong and persistent and fierce, that horrified me when I looked in the mirror, that filled me with shame, that made me feel ugly. My mother would look at me with worry-filled eyes, furrowing her brow, tsk-ing tsk-ing, as she turned my face one way and then the other, as she made a threat assessment and confirmed the importance of spending her hard-earned and carefully saved money on laser treatments. Laser treatments that might finally turn the tide and permanently remove the insurgent hair that persistently grew back, maybe even thicker, despite years of waxing and threading.

Back then, laser technology was rudimentary. Like photography and videography, laser technology was made first for white skin. This meant that the technology was less effective for brown and black skin. Another reason to curse the colour of my skin and wish it fair. The woman who administered the treatments was Pakistani. She'd bought a machine and installed it in a poorly heated strip mall store-front in Mississauga. I remember going there, all bundled up in the winter, driving through treacherous snow, on grey winter days. I'd sit in a cold waiting room or a hallway with other South Asian women, all of us hoping to rid ourselves of our unwanted hair, turn our fortunes even, if we could finally be beautiful. All of us subjecting ourselves to painful and potentially dangerous technology in order to remove hair that we believed made us look ugly, undesirable, unfuckable.

Hair that indeed did all of the things we thought it did. We weren't crazy. This was just self-preservation. We were making a calculated decision, giving ourselves the best chance for upward mobility, a good suitor. Well, at least that was true in my case. I don't know the calcula-tions of the others. But I do know it had to do with stand-ards of beauty in our overlapping communities, each one of which found female bodily hair so reprehensible that we were willing to pay a high price, both financially and physically – we didn't know or care about the long-term effects of the treatment – to remove this naturally grow-ing hair.

The laser had to be turned up really high to zap the hair on our non-white skin. As the laser machine warmed up, the technician would shave my face with a razor. This was painless. Then she'd run the laser over it, zapping the hair, making a crackling sound, leaving behind the smell of burnt hair, and red, hot, angry skin. Little bumps would pop up all over my face. I'd have to cool it for *days* with an ice pack. It was one of the few times I was grateful to wear niqab. Because if I thought that facial hair was conspicuous, imagine a swollen red face, little bumps where each and every hair follicle had been fried, hopefully killed, rendered forever inactive, dead.

Years later, when I'd get laser treatments in New York City and Vancouver, with all the new lasers that were meant to do better on dark skin, all promising hair eradication in only six treatments, the experience was just a slightly milder version of those earlier times. There was still the sting of the hair follicle being fried, the smell of burnt hair, the sound of a pop or a crackle, the reddened and swollen face that needed an icepack, the gratitude for the cooling function on the laser to settle the skin. But the redness that looked like a rash didn't last for days anymore, and the skin didn't burn or hyper pigment as much because the lasers were more sophisticated.

Eventually, I was paying for my own treatments. So the financial burden transferred from my dear mother to me, which lightened our relationship, for which I am grateful. My mother saw her spending on my laser treatments as self-sacrifice, as an act of love that I ought to recognise and for which I ought to be grateful and indebted. I want to convey

this in a way that isn't only manipulative. Really, it came
from a woman raised and living in patriarchal societies. As
a woman in a patriarchal state, Canada, my mother didn't
have access to many professional development services, such
as English language classes, available to male immigrants,
because the government of Canada assumed that immigrant women were dependent on their husbands. The
government figured that, for at least the first decade after
immigrating to Canada, immigrant women would rely on
their men to take care of the manly business of learning the
language and acquiring skills, and that such services would
be redundant for women.

And as a woman in a patriarchal relationship with her
husband, my mother could only access power through
subversive means. This is how you secured your future. Your
children are your security, your insurance. Lord knows you
won't have the financial means to care for yourself if you
don't work or speak the language. You're dependent on the
kindness of a generous husband – if you have one – and
your children, if you have them. Children must be reminded
to be grateful and indebted; this is important for your
survival. Your children's guilt, their sense of indebtedness,
that's your insurance.

And I am grateful. Indebted. Guilty.

Love comes in all forms.

1997

In university I met a Pakistani couple that had started moving toward a more conservative version of Islam, an Islam that they were beginning to see as more 'Islamic' than the Islam they were raised with in Pakistan. The wife was from a wealthy Pakistani family, and had never worn hijab before coming to Canada, but now started wearing it and was screwing up the courage to wear niqab as well. Her husband was a PhD student at the University of Toronto. He used to play guitar when he was in Pakistan, but as he became 'more religious', he put the guitar away and grew out his beard. This couple loved my parents, whom they visited often, starting with dinner, and then they'd spend the night. My parents loved them too, they cooked them elaborate meals, inviting them over and insisting that they spend the night. On Wednesdays my Economics 101 class finished at 9:00P.M., and I often spent the night in their graduate student apartment on Charles Street, sleeping on their couch. I convinced my parents that it was safer for me to do this than take the university bus home so late at night. The husband knew I loved bagels so he'd pick one up for me from Tim Hortons in the mornings. And his wife introduced me to a technology that changed my life. For a decade or so.

The Silk-épil. A battery-operated depilatory machine that removes hair by means of small metal clamps on a rotating circular tube. The horizontal tube turns as the clamps open and close. These clamps catch any hair, or

skin, they encounter, and the circular motion of the tube
tugs on the hair, pulling it out by its roots. I loved this
machine because it meant that I could remove my body hair
wherever and whenever I wanted, by myself, and in small
sections.

Waxing required assistance and a ton of prep, so much
so that it almost demanded you remove as much hair as
possible in one go. If you were going to go through the trouble of making the wax, ensuring the right consistency by
cooking it just right, applying it correctly, getting all sticky,
then you might as well wax as much as possible in one shot.
Waxing was best administered by someone else. Threading
was done by a technician who magically turned threads into
scissors, pulling hair out by its root, and sometimes accidentally cutting skin. *Ow!* you might yell suddenly, eliciting an
Oh sorry! as the aesthetician rubbed your skin lightly and
continued. Lasering required, well, a laser. Electrolysis
required a whole different machine. One with a gold needle.
The technician would slide the needle into each pore on
your face, as if sliding a hand into a pocket, and then fry
individual hair follicles.

The Silk-épil took all the prep out of the process. It
removed the need for assistance entirely. All other methods
of hair removal required someone else's help; they required
a community of sorts. The Silk-épil inverted this model; it
was easier if you were alone. Also, you didn't have to wait
for the hair to be a certain length before you pulled it out.
You didn't have to become ugly before you could be

beautiful again. You could keep up with your hair growth, removing hair in sections, from hands, forearms, calves, armpits, thighs. But what you gained in ease of use, you lost in anxious repetition. The longer your hair got, the more painful it was to remove. You needed to be on top of Silk-épiling, making sure to depilate every few days, blocking off time no matter where you were or what you were doing, knowing that each delay brought with it the promise of greater pain.

'Silk-épil' was always on my to-do list. As I'd rattle off my plan for the day to Rumee I'd often say, . . . *and I need to Silk-épil!*

And though I was made weary by the endless and eternal nature of this task, much like Sisyphus pushing a rock up the hill, I engaged in it with religious regularity.

2015

We are all inheritors. We inherit traditions, religions, cultures and social customs. We inherit ideas of beauty and ugliness. Of morality and virtue. Of good and bad. Of what is civilised and what is barbaric. Of what is sophisticated and what is primitive. It is all intertwined, entangled, wrapped up together in our art, in our curriculum and in our markets. We make our way in the world by negotiating our inheritance. Cherishing some parts, abandoning others, reshaping parts that don't quite fit but that we want to keep anyway. Our relationship with our inheritance changes over time. We might reject an inheritance at first but then come to love it. And the other way around, too. What we inherit is both abstract and tangible. We inherit physical bodies, traits, proclivities, diseases. And also mannerisms, beliefs, memories, skills, traumas and joys.

One of the things Rumee inherited from his family is male pattern baldness. And also, a fear of balding and a sorrow for it. At some point, usually in their thirties, males in his family begin to lose their hair. This particular inheritance is a gift from Rumee's maternal grandfather. It was passed down to Rumee's mother, and then from mother to son. Rumee lived his life in fear of this inevitability. He did not want to lose his hair. Since we became friends and lovers, in our early twenties, male pattern baldness has been an ever-present, underlying anxiety. Rumee's hair was beautiful and thick, and he grew it out long, so that it fell around his face in pretty locks. It was wavy and luscious. He loved his hair. Likely more so because of its impending loss.

And I loved his hair too, and felt his pain, and dreaded, with him, the loss of his hair.

What will I do? he'd wonder.

What will you do? I'd wonder.

Rumee fully expected science and the medical profession to come through for him, to help him avoid the fate of the rest of the men in his family, his ancestors, to escape this plague in his genealogy. So when his hair began to thin, we began visiting doctors. We considered invasive procedures, like hair implants, taking hair from one part of his body and implanting it on to his head. He was pretty serious about it. We met for a consultation with a famous doctor from New York, who also had a practice in Vancouver. It was all going well, the doctor was talking up the procedure, until he learned of Rumee's keloids, which are spontaneous fatty deposits that sometimes appear on his skin, looking like scars left over from a knife fight. The doctor said that the hair implant procedure was not good for someone with keloids, so he wouldn't do it.

Rumee was dejected. He really wanted the procedure to save his hair. He felt his body was conspiring against him, when it was actually trying to save him. Because, of course, there is nothing objectively wrong with losing one's hair. It is not a disease, it is not a deficiency, it is not a plague. It doesn't hurt, it is not painful. The only reason that hair loss is undesirable is aesthetic. Rumee had been taught, by society, by family, by movies, that bald men are aesthetically less pleasing, less beautiful, less virile, less manly. And the fact that none of this is true is beside the point.

The New York doctor in Vancouver told Rumee he couldn't help him with hair implants, but he did encourage him to take Propecia pills to help slow down the hair loss, and maybe even stop it altogether. Rumee was worried about side effects. He didn't want to become sick trying to save his hair. The doctor was dismissive. He waved his hand, quickly, swatting away legitimate concerns as if they were flies in his face, and said, *MILLIONS of men are on Propecia. If it was harmful, we'd know about it.*

He also recommended Rogaine, a topical solution that could work in tandem with the oral medication, to save his hair. Rumee bought boxes of Rogaine, and he'd carefully apply it to his head every morning and every night, with desperate hopes and prayers for a miracle, a reversal of hair loss, the preservation of hair. Pretty soon, the skin on his ears started to peel, and his scalp became itchy and red – he said it felt as if it was on fire. Turns out this is a possible side effect of Rogaine. Apparently, it might help you keep your hair, but in return, you'd be miserable in your skin. What a bargain! Rumee stuck with it for a few months, despite the burning of his scalp and ears, taking a chance at fulfilling a particular vision of beauty in his mind while feeling more and more at dis-ease in his skin. Finally, he could not bear it anymore.

Fuck it, he told me, *I'm not doing this Rogaine shit anymore. God knows what else it is doing to my body.*

Yes, stop! I worried with him, for him.

But he kept up with the Propecia. It wasn't having immediately visible side effects. Months passed and Rumee descended into a deep depression. He became moody and withdrawn. He used to be full of a lightness, an easy joy. Now, he was unhappy, discontent. He said he couldn't keep a thought straight in his head. I had trouble recognising him. It can be difficult to spot depression when you're in it, or if you are too close to someone in it. I knew that

Rumee was acting differently, but I didn't know that he was depressed. I remember spending a picture-perfect day on the beach with him and my sister. We had the day to ourselves, the sun was shining and the water was a glorious blue-green, the waves were majestic. Normally, Rumee would have been ecstatic. He's the one who taught me to love a day like this. But today, he was sitting away from us. At one point I looked over at him and saw that he had a towel on his head to shield him from the sun. When I called to him he looked up, skin deeply tanned, a bright white towel on his head and a face full of such misery that it closed in on itself. Instead of opening his face to accept the kisses of the sun, he was turning away, from love, from light.

We stumbled through the darkness of his depression together, me trying imperfectly and inadequately to hold him up, to pull him along. It didn't occur to me that he was clinically depressed. At some point, he figured it out himself. He knew something was very wrong. He looked up the side effects of Propecia and there it was, in tiny print on the back of a small strip of paper found stuck to the inside of the box: *Side effects may include depression and suicidal ideation.* And then he told me that he had been fantasising about killing himself, about jumping off our balcony. And other horrific thoughts. Graphic fantasies of suicide. He said it had become almost an obsession, an itch that he worried he would not be able to resist. He was so certain he might commit suicide that he wrote up all the passwords for various accounts and put them in our safety deposit box at the bank for me to find after he had passed. So I wouldn't suffer the hardship of not being able to get into our accounts.

I was shocked to learn this. Terrified.

Don't you think that your death would be a far greater hardship for me than not having access to our accounts?! I asked, at once angry and scared of the answer.

He stopped taking the fucking Propecia and the depression dissolved, slowly, over the next few weeks and months. Sizzling out, leaving behind a lingering scent, a trail, a reminder of the horrors that could have been.

On his thirty-fifth birthday, we were in Los Angeles. We went for a lovely hike off the Pacific Coast Highway, climbing hills that overlooked the ocean. Huge waves crashed on to the beach below as the clouds rose and lifted around us, thinning out in places and showing us the ocean, then thickening around us, enveloping us completely. The brown shrubbery, with the bright purple and orange flowers, changed dramatically against the ocean and blue sky or white grey clouds. The same place looked different, smelled different, felt different, within a matter of seconds. It was as if the earth was reminding us, teaching us, that we are always changing, from moment to moment. Change is part of us. It is essential to us. It is the only constant in life. Nothing stands still.

When we finished the hike and returned to the city, we went straight to a salon and Rumee had his head shaved. We both watched him in the mirror as his hair fell off in clumps, as his perfectly shaped skull emerged from beneath his hair.

It looks kind of badass, he said, shyly, tentatively, trying out the words.

Yes! You do *look badass!* I agreed enthusiastically.

Over time, the pale skin on his head tanned to a golden brown, matching his face and neck. He has a particular look when his head is freshly shaved, and then it changes on day one and day two and week one and week two of growth. Each look feels different under my hand, rough little bumps of hair that grow to be soft and fuzzy, moving from a gentle scratch to a caress when, in the mornings, he curls into my arms, snuggling into my neck.

We have come to love, truly love, his shaved head.

I almost lost him because he was trying to save his hair. Because he was trying his best to avoid what we now love. Because he was trying to be beautiful, when he already was.

962 BCE

Depilatory methods are ancient.

Human hair is natural, our bodies evolved in this way. It is what is animal about us. It reminds us of our kinship with non-human animals. And it is a uniquely human trait to try to distance ourselves from this kinship, by erasing, rearranging, altering our hair, using increasingly sophisticated methods. Our relationship with the hair on our heads, on our faces, on our genitals, on our limbs, changes with time and place. Sometimes facial hair for men is 'masculine', other times it is not manly enough; sometimes it is read as extremist and other times it is read as hipster. Same with hair on the head – sometimes it is a sign of virility, other times it is a sign of weakness. A hairstyle can be beautiful and uncouth at the same time, depending on context. In the United States, black girls are expelled from schools for sporting natural hairstyles. They are punished for just letting their hair be, which is to say for just being. In France, women are expelled from public spaces for covering their hair. In Iran, women are prosecuted for uncovering their hair. Hair is heavily policed. Hair is political.

Sulayman (King Solomon) was outraged when he learned, from the hoopoe bird, that the land of Sheba was ruled over by a queen. The very existence of an independent kingdom made him insecure, but then to find out that this competing, thriving, flourishing kingdom was ruled by a woman proved too much to bear. It boggled his mind that this Queen was not monotheistic, that she worshipped the sun, which nourished the earth, created food and showed up every morning, rather than an abstract and invisible god whom Sulayman said had personally chosen him to be Prophet and King. So Sulayman set about trying to subdue the Queen, to gain dominance over her. In the end he was able to dominate her, but the story behind that domination is puzzling.

He started by demanding that the Queen submit herself to his rule. The Queen responded by sending Sulayman gifts and good wishes, which were rebuffed and returned with threats of war. To stave off war, the Queen visited Sulayman in the hopes of resolving their conflict through diplomacy. But when she arrived at his palace, she made a critical mistake. As she entered his court, she mistook the smooth, polished glass floor for water and raised her skirt to avoid getting wet; in raising her skirt, she exposed her shins. Rather than a small, laughable misunderstanding, this turned out to be a grave error, because when Sulayman corrected her, explaining that she stood on polished glass rather than water, she said,

My Lord, indeed I have zalamtu nafsi [transgressed against myself]! I submit with Sulayman to Allah, Lord of the worlds.

She became a monotheist. Traded the sun for the invisible god. Why? What was so egregious about her mistaking glass for water that she had to cede her political authority on the spot?

The Qur'an doesn't tell us, but medieval Muslim scholars pondered over it and came up with a theory. They borrowed heavily from their Jewish counterparts, who inherited a very similar story, and said that the Queen's error was not that she mistook glass for water, but that when she raised her skirt, she exposed her shins, and in doing so inadvertently revealed that she had hairy legs. They said that the hair on her legs compromised her beauty – it was a monstrosity, an ugliness, a weakness. It was unfeminine, like

the fact of her rule to begin with. Women were not supposed
to be rulers, they said. Her very rule upset the patriarchal,
monotheistic worldview that medieval scholars took for
granted. God didn't choose women to be rulers, He chose
men. He was a 'he', and so men, being male, were de facto
closer to the divine, more God-like by virtue of their male-
ness. A queen, a ruler with a vagina and a womb and lack-
ing a penis, upset the order of the universe. Her hairy legs
confirmed what everyone already knew, and broadcast to
the court that, *There is something wrong here.*

Her hairy legs exposed her unnatural masculinity, her
unruliness, her ugliness. Some of these men, these medieval
Muslim and Jewish scholars reflecting on the story, went
even further. They had such a low opinion of women that
they didn't believe that any woman, not even a manly one,
could ever be a successful ruler of a thriving empire. So they
made up stories about her being a half-demon, that she was
the spawn of a beautiful woman and a demon having fucked,
upsetting the 'natural' order of the universe further. Her
hairy legs proved this, for though she inherited her face
from her mother, her legs were her father's. Her hairy legs
were demonic.

So great was the power of a woman's hairy legs in the
minds of these men that it extinguished her political power
in one fell swoop. And these men believed that it was after
this moment that women began depilating their hair, having
seen how deeply compromising it was. The towering Queen
of Sheba, a woman who ruled over a flourishing empire so

magnificent that it threatened Sulayman, was thus reduced to the Queen of Depilation.

2010

I know the feminist literature on shaving, on removing hair, on how doing so fulfils specific racialised and gendered constructions of beauty. It's the part of the literature I find myself ignoring. I respect women who don't shave. But I've thoroughly absorbed, internalised, the idea that I am only beautiful when I am hairless, that I am beautiful and clean and good when I've made my skin hairless and smooth. I feel better, to the touch, to *me*. I smell better to *me*. The hair in my armpit holds on to odour that I'm free of when I've removed it. I can smell the difference on myself. I 'look' better to *myself*. I think Rumee finds me more attractive when I remove my bodily hair, though he denies it, says he'd love me just the same if I didn't. But I believe he's as weighed down by this inheritance as I am.

The hijab and niqab did not protect me from the pressures of society's aesthetic preferences, from the beauty standards set for women. I remember an NYU professor's surprise at learning that I was anorexic. He said, *I thought that with your hijab, you would have escaped the demands of beauty standards.*

I wanted to, but didn't say, *Why would you think that? I'm still a person in the world, I see the same billboards and magazine covers as everyone else!*

I know how people see me. I know how people would look at me if I walked into a swimming pool or a sauna, or down the street or into a restaurant in shorts and a T-shirt with all my hair intact, natural. People would be disgusted, they would cringe, they would wrinkle their noses, look away. They might even say something, who knows? But they wouldn't have to. We communicate with our bodies, first and foremost. Much less so with our words.

All my life, I have confronted the repulsed human gaze. The gaze that looks away in pity, in disgust, in horror, in anger. When I wore hijab and niqab, I encountered this gaze on a daily basis. I always assumed that when I stopped wearing them, I would stop facing social ostracism for how I carried my body. For how I presented it and how I covered it. And now, as I imagine walking around with my hairy legs and arms and face, I can see the same looks of pity, and horror, and disgust, and anger focused on me.

In the end, it is as simple as this: instead of being repulsive, I want to be desired, to be desirable. I live in this world. In this world, hairy women aren't desirable. Well, that's not true. Men and women and gender non-binary people do find women in their natural state, with their hair intact, desirable. But we hardly ever hear about it. The narrative of the hairless female body as beautiful is so strong, it erases all other desires, pushes them to the margins, makes them almost unbelievable.

2016

A few years ago, I switched to bleaching the hair on my face, on my upper neck and under my chin. I had less hair there than I used to, so bleaching sort of did the job. The golden hair blended in with my skin tone better than the black hair so that you wouldn't notice it unless you looked closely. I met a friend for lunch one afternoon, and was telling him about my day. As I listed the things I'd done that day, I said, . . . *and then I bleached my face, and then* . . .

He's African American, and it matters for this story, because for a couple of beats, he stared at me, alarmed and confused. I quickly specified, *Oh no, I didn't bleach the* skin *on my face, I bleached the* hair *on my face!* We laughed raucously at the misunderstanding. Soon after, I wondered if we had been laughing at different things: me at his thinking I was bleaching the skin on my face instead of the hair, him at my thinking there was a qualitative difference between the two.

The conversation left me unsettled. Could I be wrong about all this? Dare I imagine that I might be beautiful, desirable, lovable, good, just as I am, in my natural state, without any alterations, without the hair removed from my legs and arms and hands and armpits, my pubic hair shaved or trimmed, my facial hair bleached, the hair on my head dyed black #3? I'm not sure I dare imagine it.

2018

Turns out imagination is important. Vital. If you cannot imagine a thing, it cannot be. And so it is with my hair. I could not imagine it as beautiful in its natural form, though I tried. Not anywhere. Not on my head, and not on my body. For six months, I grew out the hair all over my body. All of it. I didn't colour the hair on my head, nor did I trim or remove hair from anywhere. I let it all grow out. And I could not see myself as beautiful. I only saw ugliness.

White hair sprouted on my head, right in the centre, thick and coarse, ageing me, making me look far older than I wanted. I tried to cover it by parting my hair farther and farther to the left, so that the black hair would cover the white hair, but it would always slip. When I looked in the mirror, I'd be reminded of my age, of my mortality, of my degenerating body. And I'd look away, avoiding my own reflection. I wonder, if I didn't see my reflection, would my hair bother me less? Would I have less trouble letting it grow natural?

And the hair on my body, well, it grew out and was as unseemly as I remembered it. Even though it had thinned out somewhat over the years, there was still too much of it. It covered my thighs and shins and toes and forearms. Rumee assured me that he found me beautiful and attractive with all my hair. I believed him this time.

But I carried an abstract social gaze, a constructed aesthetic within me; this gaze spoke to me, in my head, in my body, it whispered over and over and over again that the hair on my body was unattractive. God speaks to us loudly and clearly, but Satan whispers, he speaks in waswasa. The waswasa of Shaytan is sneaky; to avoid accountability, it hides itself from us, even as it buries itself deep inside us. Now, I heard the waswasa and I covered myself. For whom? Why did I care? I avoided wearing shorts and dresses, afraid to break a social code about hair on the female form. I noticed all the women around me who were hairless.

I saw a little girl playing in the water fountain in New York City's Washington Square Park on a sunny and hot afternoon. Her mother changed her clothes in the park, removing them all before putting on new ones. She must have been about three. As I watched, I realised I hated that little girl's body. Her shamelessness exposed my shame. And I knew in that moment that, despite all my efforts to love myself, I hated my body.

When I got back to Vancouver, I got the hair on my head coloured, and I made an appointment at a laser hair removal centre. This is the most professional place I've been to so far for hair removal; it has a medical aesthetic rather than a spa aesthetic. The white technician who administered my first treatment walked me through the process. She told me that because I was dark-skinned, they would have to use the highest setting on a laser that they called 'the mean machine'.

It will be painful, she warned me. *Basically, the laser goes through three layers of skin and burns the root of each hair follicle. Normally, this would happen only if all three layers of skin were burned off. So, your body is going to think that that is what is happening, and it will freak out. But the pain you will feel is just imaginary, because that is not happening. So, you have to remember that, okay? Your pain is not real. It is mental, it is in your head.*

She recommended that I apply two tubes of Emla, a topical anaesthetic to my legs and armpits and face in preparation for the treatment. I chose not to do so the first time. I didn't want the extra poison, even though I was willing to be lasered. The folly of this bargain is not lost on me.

Rumee felt very conflicted about my decision to remove my hair permanently. He didn't want me to do it, but he also acknowledged that he didn't know what it felt like to be a woman whose hair was considered repulsive, revolting to others. So, he wanted to get over himself to support me. He offered to come with me to the appointment. I agreed, glad for his support, as yet unaware of how much I would need him.

We entered the little room where the treatment would take place. There was a large exhaust pipe over the table to catch the smell of burnt hair and smoke. The technician gave me two stress balls, one for each hand. And glasses to protect my eyes. And then the treatment began. Over 2,500 laser zaps on my legs and armpits and face. It hurt more than anything I have ever experienced. My body shuddered and quaked. Rumee held my upper arms, which were stretched over my head. I asked him to pinch me, hurt me on my arms to distract me from the liquid fire pouring over my legs. My arms were getting bruised and I needed him to bruise me more in order to withstand the pain.

Rumee tried to joke, *You could walk right out of here and into a police station, and report me for abuse.*

Yeah, but I'm still a woman. There's a one in five chance they'd dismiss my claim, I shot back.

The technician talked throughout the two-hour treatment. She told me to direct my anger toward my hair.

Die, motherfuckers, die! she screamed. *Don't come back!*

And then, *As far as I know, Islam is the only religion founded by a warlord.*

What the fuck?! I yelled, exasperated, depleted of all patience for bullshit.

She told me she learned that in a course on world religions at the University of British Columbia a few years ago, when she went back to finish her degree. Some of what we inherit is just trash.

I sweated on that table, I writhed in pain. Afterwards, I was quiet, exhausted, cleansed. I told my therapist about my experience, *Honestly, I feel like it cleansed me, like I was purified.*

Oh, I'm sure it did, she responded, *but there are better ways to purify yourself than torture.*

My skin was hot for days after the treatment. It was tender for weeks. Little round circles the shape of the laser strikes lingered on my skin. The next three times I went back for the treatment, I had another, kinder, gentler technician. This white woman did not denigrate my religion, but she did insist that the pain was all in my head. And I applied the topical anaesthetic, which made the treatments slightly more bearable. But it was still so painful as to be torturous. The technician warned me not to use more than two bottles of topical anaesthetic because it could be dangerous.

Did you hear the story of the girl who used four bottles before her treatment? She died in the cab on the way to the clinic.

They gave me an Atavan to calm my nerves. And a Motrin to help with the pain. And I found a place deep inside myself where, for several moments at a time, I could actually escape the pain. Rumee came with me to all the treatments, and massaged my feet.

He and the technician talked, and I moved in and out of myself, hearing only snippets of their conversation. She told us about her husband, who used to be her music teacher between ninth and twelfth grade. She told us about her in-laws. And she asked me, *Do you like your bum hair?* as she zapped a few hairs there.

The last time I saw her, I said, *I know this is fucked up, that I'm doing this. Removing hair that grows naturally. I've internalised the perverse message that I'm only beautiful when I'm hairless.*

But it also feels really nice, she said, *when you've removed the hair and can feel the skin. It feels clean.*

She told me about how she found a sex manual from the sixties in her parents' home when she was young, and the women in the images all had hair where she had none. And it made her worried, because she didn't have as much hair as the women. She thought something was wrong with her. It made me wonder if all representations of humans are harmful, because they can never represent everyone. Will every representation of humans marginalise some people who do not see themselves reflected in the image? Are all representations bad? Maybe Islam was on to something with its wariness around representational art.

At the end of each treatment, my body shivered, my teeth chattered, my legs twitched involuntarily, my toes sweated. I was cold. I was hot. Rumee rubbed aloe vera on the freshly lasered, red-hot skin. My skin was bruised for weeks. And still, I returned.

Here's the thing about inheritance. You might disown it but it can still claim you.

And also this: just because you know better doesn't mean you do better.

2020

I don't laser anymore, or Silk-épil, or thread, or wax, or bleach my hair. I'm even growing out the white hair on my head. Or, rather, I'm letting my hair be. Sometimes I shave the hair on my arms, but not very often. When I look at my almost hairless legs and armpits, I feel an unexpected sorrow. I should be happy that I prevailed over my hair, that I finally killed the follicles it grew from so I don't have to keep removing it. But instead, I feel a sense of loss. Like I broke something inside me. Finally, and too late, I wonder, was that a good idea, to make it so my hair doesn't grow? After all, hair grows on living bodies. It doesn't grow on dead ones.

I succeeded at this endless, repetitive task by paying the price for imposing order on my body, so it could be clean and beautiful. And yet. This success feels like failure. And it makes me think, why do mathematicians call patterns and order beautiful? What if beauty is in the chaos, in the unstructured, in the untidy, in the unclean?

God says, وإن تعدوا نعمة الله لا تحصوها

If you try to count the blessings of God, you will never be able to enumerate them.

I always thought this meant that God's blessings were so many that human numbers could never encompass them. But what if it really means that we are unable to count the blessings of God because they are uncountable, they defy enumeration? Applying a number to a blessing reduces it, so maybe numbers can never help us reckon with the blessings of God. And further still, what if as soon as we enumerate them, they stop being blessings? Because as soon we enumerate them, we possess them in a kind of way, and God's blessings can never be possessed, only enjoyed. What if the problem is with the counting to begin with? Accepting the blessings of God means accepting them as they are, as perfect in their natural form, uncounted and uncountable, unaltered. In which case, perfection comes not from our mind imposing our ideas of perfection outside of itself, but rather from submitting to the perfections all around us. What if the only way we know we've encountered beauty is when we know, when we can finally rest in the knowledge, that we no longer need to count, and correct, and measure, and align, and straighten, and civilise, and clean? What if the only way to be clean is knowing we are already clean? When we can finally hear God's voice ringing loud and clear:

لا تبديل لخلق الله

Let there be no change in God's creation.

Children

Rumee and I decided not to have children. The decision sort of emerged for us slowly over the years, in stages, some unplanned. We took it one step at a time, went with the flow, so that now, in our forties and almost twenty years into our partnership, we know that we will not have children. Biological or adopted.

When we were younger and people learned that we didn't plan on having children, their responses were rather dramatic.

Oh no! Why?! they wanted to know.

Your poor parents! they'd worry.

But your children would be SO beautiful!

They'd have SUCH great hair!

YOU'RE the kind of people who NEED to have kids!

But your kids would be SO smart!

The presumptuousness of these comments might make you think that these people were close friends. But to the contrary, we'd only just met. They didn't know much about us, they certainly had no clue as to what kind of parents we'd be, because, well, they didn't know us.

These days the reactions we get are far less dramatic. Probably because we are older. People are less sad about us not having children and we're less defensive. Now, the conversation goes like this:

Do you have children?
No.
Huh.

I was always struck by the invasive, overly familiar nature of the questions I received, and occasionally still receive, for not having children. Apart from being annoying, they're weird. Why is everyone expected to have kids? Why are we all expected to love child rearing? And why aren't there licensing requirements for having a kid, like mandatory parenting classes, the way we have for driving a car? When I asked these questions out loud, a friend worried about the racial and class implications of obtaining licences for having children. He makes a fair point. And I don't want to create yet another way to systemically discriminate against those who are marginalised. But if there were a way to circumvent discrimination – I know, I know, but *if* there were – then there could be a basic curriculum for child rearing, with modules like 'Don't torture your children: Ten ways to break the trauma cycle'. What I'm saying is, in my experience, good parenting is not intuitive. I've seen some truly shit parents in my life who would have benefitted from at least some amount of training. You know what I'm talking about.

I'm genuinely intrigued by the people who pity us, who use passive-aggressive comments to shame us for not having children.

Oh, poor you! You'll never know what it feels like to love someone so completely.

I'm so sad you won't have this experience. Children are amazing! You learn so much from them.

There's a special connection between moms and their kids!

Parenting gives me such a unique and special perspective.

Oh, you wouldn't get it, it's a mom thing!

And then, some time later, usually in the same conversation, a switch flips and the same people, the very same people, might say:

Oh my god! What a smart idea to not have kids! You don't know how hard it is. I don't have a life anymore. I forgot what it feels like to sleep five hours straight.

No wonder you're so happy! It must be nice. It's so hard to do anything with kids. I can't even pee in peace anymore. Or take a shower.

My children are trying to destroy us. We never have sex anymore.

Childbirth changed my body. Nothing is where it used to be, nobody told me that would happen. Everything moved!

Really? Wow. If I had to go back in time, I don't know that I'd do it again. I mean, don't get me wrong, I love my kids, but if I went back in time . . .

Their voices trail off as they get a vacant look in their eyes.

It's that flip that fascinates me, because, presumably, these people know that they have misgivings about having children before the conversation begins. Their laments are fine on their own, and I sympathise, except that they are preceded by a concerted, perhaps even desperate attempt to convince me otherwise. Why the need to hide one's regrets? Why not lead with them, or at least discuss parenthood in a more complex way?

I understand there is a special bond between mothers and their children. This is a bond I will never understand from a mother's perspective given that I am not a mother, though of course I do understand this bond from a child's perspective given that I have a mother. It's also true that couples who have children will never know what it feels like to be in a long-term partnership, where you get to sleep for eight to ten hours on most nights, and have long, uninterrupted conversations. That's a pretty amazing bond, too. And one that would simply not exist, that we would have missed out on, if we'd had children. But being childless is not for everyone. Just like having children isn't for everyone.

Ultimately, I think, conversations about children are actually conversations about loneliness, and mortality, and the meaning of life. Do I like myself enough to be alone with myself? What if I am alone and lonely when I grow old? Who will remember me when I die? What is the purpose of my life? Is there any point to my ever having been here? At some point, every one of us has to confront these questions, grapple with them, answer them for ourselves, come to terms with our choices in the face of them. But most of us try to find a way around these questions, we avoid them for as long as possible; we will go to great lengths to avoid asking and answering these questions for ourselves. Sometimes we produce whole human beings to distract us from these questions. We treat the questions like they are fire, like they will burn us and leave nothing behind. But there is no way around the fire, only through it. And though fire can be destructive, it can also be purifying. It can clear way for new life, it can preserve what is already standing, it can reveal the core of a thing. Fire is a teacher. One of the things the fire has taught me is that what we consider nightmarish can become a source of deep peace and comfort. Loneliness is terrifying until being alone is a solace. And the insignificance of our lives is scary until we see how this truth sets us free.

I always thought I would have children. I was raised to believe it was my purpose in life. Israr Ahmed, for all his disagreements with Maulana Maududi about democracy, was in full agreement with him about the purpose of women: they were *baby-making machines*. I knew what I was supposed to do, what I was meant to do.

When I was a teenager, I couldn't wait to get married and have kids. I remember being impatient for the married and motherhood part of my life to just start already. It's what grown-ups did. They got married and had kids. And I wanted to be a grown-up.

Then I went to university and learned about individualism, autonomy, free will, the rights of the individual versus the rights of the community, feminism, women's rights over their bodies – all the basic tenets of liberalism, taught and promoted as unadulterated goods. My imaginative horizons began to expand. I imagined a future where I went to graduate school and earned a PhD and became a professor. Suddenly, marriage and children went from being the only option, to being obstacles in the path of this new future. In my teens and early twenties, I was engaged three times, to three separate men. Another story for another time. All three men saw my dreams of a PhD and a career as obstacles to their own dreams of marriage and children. One ex-fiancé asked, *Why do you need to study Islam with the kuffar anyways? What are you going to learn from them? And when you're away studying and working, what about my needs? I have needs!*

Well, I was never able to attend to any of his needs, because we never got married.

When Rumee and I started courting, we were pretty fundamentalist, so we made sure to be clear – with each other and with ourselves – that we were engaging in conversation solely for the purpose of determining whether we should get married, and this made space for us to talk frankly about what kind of marriage we envisioned for ourselves. Still, it was a difficult conversation to have because we barely knew each other. We were shy and ashamed, uncomfortable talking about procreation, which is to say, sex. The legal principle, *la haya fi-l-islam* (*there is no shame in Islam*) gave us the courage to have the conversation anyways. So we talked about sex. We would use birth control. I would have control over my body. I would get a veto over my uterus. I would decide whether to have kids or not – though, of course, we would make the decision in a consultative manner. But if we were ever at an impasse, we agreed that my desire to not have children would override Rumee's desire to have them.

Six months after our wedding, my nephew died. I loved him. I still love him. A lot. There was nothing wrong with him. He wasn't ill. His heart just stopped. His death rattled me. You could do everything right. Have a baby in a modern hospital with all the latest technology. When he gets sick, take him to a modern hospital with all the latest technology. And he could still die. The experience of losing someone I loved so much was harrowing and I went into a deep depression.

I was newly married, living in a new city, with no friends or family close by, with in-laws who had disowned Rumee for marrying me. In-laws who did not like me. People comforted us by saying that they'd come around once we had kids.

Just wait and see. They're gonna want to see their grandkids!

IF we have kids, we'd say.

Oh, you'll have kids!

But I didn't want to have children just to make Rumee's parents accept him, accept me. I mean, how fucked up would that be? Create a whole new human being just so that parents who were, at the time, parenting poorly, would start speaking to their son again. Didn't really make a lot of sense to me.

A few years passed. I was on birth control. Yasmin and then Yaz. Both had terrible side effects and became the subject of multiple class action lawsuits. I was insanely hormonal on the pill. My breasts, which I always believed were too large to begin with as B cups, grew to double Ds. I hated them. I had dramatic mood swings. Rumee worried about all the hormones I was putting in my body every day. Then, six years into our marriage, while we were in Los Angeles for the summer, Rumee found a 'vasectomist to the stars' and booked an appointment. His insurance covered the elective surgery, so he paid only $250 for it. The insurance didn't cover my birth control, nor would it cover abortions or the surgery for getting my tubes tied. But it covered vasectomies. It's good to be a man. Not just in Islam.

Given that Rumee and I usually discuss major decisions ad nauseam before taking any steps, it came as a surprise to both of us that, when we tried to talk about his vasectomy, we had very little to say. He'd bring it up, *So, I'm thinking of getting a vasectomy. I don't like all the hormones you're taking. And since we're unlikely to have kids . . .*

Sure, makes sense . . . Are you sure you want a vasectomy? What if we change our minds?

Will we, though?

Probably not.

By this time, I was pretty sure I wasn't interested in producing a child with my body. Nothing about pregnancy or childbirth appealed to me. Not the growing belly, not the waddling, not the difficulty in finding a comfortable sleeping position, not the pain, trauma and suffering of childbirth, the ripping apart of the body, the shitting in front of everyone during the delivery. I hate needles and any medical contact. So, no, I wasn't planning on producing and delivering a baby with my body. We were still open to adoption, in case I got 'egg-y', which everyone kept promising would happen. It never did. Shows how much everyone knows.

Rumee went to the doctor for his consultation. By his telling, it was a pretty straightforward procedure. It would take about fifteen minutes. And though it was technically reversible, it really wasn't. The doctor was going to cut his vas deferens, cauterise the ends and clamp them shut with titanium.

Better not do this unless you're a hundred per cent sure, the doctor advised Rumee.

And then he asked to meet with me to make sure I consented to this procedure. That was when I really understood just how wrong it was for someone to have that kind of power over someone else's body. Sure, it made me feel powerful to provide consent for Rumee to do something with his own body, but it also felt deeply wrong. People should make their own decisions about whether they want to have children or not. No one else's consent should be necessary.

Rumee said the procedure went smoothly. He barely felt anything. I was in the pharmacy on the ground floor of the outpatient facility searching for a 'Happy Vasectomy!' card when he walked up behind me. I was surprised at how quickly it went. Actually fifteen minutes, as advertised. He was sore for weeks after, walking slowly, waddling up and down Abbot Kinney Boulevard. Mostly, he sat in our studio, looked out at the ocean and wrote his first book. I took up yoga that summer and have practised it since. It's been over a decade since the vasectomy and we haven't regretted it yet.

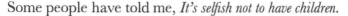

Some people have told me, *It's selfish not to have children.*

As if having children isn't selfish. People have children because they want them. So what's wrong with not having them if you don't want them? Why is one more selfish than the other? People have children to replicate their genes, leave a legacy, pass on their wealth. People have children to keep them company, to stave off loneliness; they have them because they're looking for a project, a hobby, a diversion. People have children as an insurance plan, so someone will care for them and about them in their old age. I've been asked, *Don't you worry about getting old and not having children? Who will care for you, visit you in the nursing home, pay for the nursing home?*

Yes, I worry about that, but I also know that children are a bad insurance policy. Many children leave their parents to fend for themselves, abdicating any and all responsibility. And to create a whole human being to be your caretaker? That sounds quite selfish to me. And then there's the unequal distribution of wealth and consumption and the carbon footprint of children in middle and upper class families – it's impossible to pretend that having a middle or upper class child in Canada or the United States is some kind of gift to humanity. If *I wanted children* is reason enough, then *I didn't want them* should be reason enough, too.

In the end, I did not have children for many reasons. Some of them are only becoming clear to me now. Here are some.

1. I enjoy the company of kids. I love spending time with my nieces and nephews and godchildren. But I also like giving them back.
2. I don't want to worry about them for the rest of my life. Especially with climate change. I mean, my god, what world will they inherit? A world I am afraid to see.
3. Ethically, I feel virtuous about not burdening the earth with another person.
4. It exhausts me to think of the work that goes into responsibly raising a child.
5. Children are expensive.
6. I'm afraid – no, I am certain, that I would fuck them up.
7. Long ago, I read a story about a woman in her forties who said there wasn't room in her parents' relationship

for her, an only child. I wonder if our child would feel this way.

8. I love my body too much. I don't want to put it through pregnancy and childbirth.

9. I hate my body enough to not want to experience it, confront it in this way, through pregnancy and childbirth.

10. My relationship with my mother. It makes me think that I would have a difficult relationship with my daughter. It feels inevitable. My mother and I, we love each other, and we talk, but never about what is most important, most dear to us.

11. My father. Watching him, I have learned that surviving is not the same as thriving. The horrors, the sorrows of the past never leave your body. They lie in wait, gathering strength, biding their time, as you move through the world, doing and making work, creating children and then working, toiling to feed them, provide for them. The horrors, the sorrows, they play along, let you pretend, pretend along with you, that they've been resolved, that time has healed them, that they happened so long ago, so far in the past, how could they possibly hurt with any kind of freshness? But the horrors, the sorrows have all the time in the world, to visit and revisit you, to remind you, to become your present. Occasionally, over the years, they signal their presence, remind you that they are still there, still lurking around, in a dream maybe, from which you wake making a

sound like drowning – not the finely tuned voice of human speech, but a much earlier, primordial sound, a sound of terror, a sound that knows the animal, the animal fear, in us. And then, when you finally have a moment's pause, a respite from the work, the labour of surviving, of feeding, of providing, when you finally have time to rest and do not need to wake in the dark hours for work, when your body can rest from the toil on an oil rig, or in a nuclear power plant, when the days and nights are finally yours, and you live in a house that is yours, and your children are grown, the horrors, the sorrows rise up within you, show you their home inside of you, they undo your work, they unmap you. They take, they bring you back, erase your memories starting from the last ones, so now the present becomes the past and the past is the present and you are a little boy whose brother was murdered, you are a little boy running with his family, jumping on trains, chaos around him, living in makeshift, spontaneous refugee camps, fleeing with his family, fleeing the violence, searching, searching, searching for home, for a place where he can be safe.

12. Sometimes they die.

If you decide not to have children, you might spend so much time defending your decision to your loved ones and to strangers and to yourself that you may forget that you deserve to mourn the loss that comes with not having children. To have made a decision, the right decision for you, maybe, but even in the best of circumstances, a decision that is marked by absence. The absence of the social construct of a 'complete family', of following a normative social script, of your own childhood dreams for yourself. Even if you now believe that the construct of the family, especially the nuclear family, is a myth, you still have to, at some point, contend with its loss, the death of the myth, which is the death of a dream: an attractive, unbelievable, fantastical, simple and perfect dream.

You also have to contend with the failure, if you have a uterus, of your body fulfilling its own dream, its own planning for the future. Month after month, my body lines my uterus, makes a snug, welcoming home for a little one that never arrives; and month after month, she lays waste to that cosy and safe home, throwing it all away, wiping the slate clean. Sometimes, I can feel her disappointment, pulling and pushing me at once, into the earth. But still, she doesn't give up. She keeps trying, month after month, for decades on end, to coax my child into existence. Our bodies mourn, so we must mourn too. Mourn the children that never were. The children that could have been, but aren't. And yet, here they are, because they've been conjured, over and over again, by our bodies, by our minds, by our hearts. They might have names and personalities, a particular laugh, you may have conversations with them, disagreements even.

My children are fine-boned, beautiful little rascals. They are brown. Their names are Rumana Smith and Musa Jones. And Rahma, the one who came first and helped me conjure her siblings. She has big hair, a cackling laugh, and eyes that glint with budmashi.

Perhaps it is better that they are never born into this world, that they remain safe and happy, laughing in the wombs of our imaginations.

The bird is in
your hands, Daddy said, *How you live*
your life can be the child you never had
                    —Nikky Finney, 'Linea Nigra'

PART III

'Please Water Me'

They are important, the rituals we devise around burials, around returning the body to the earth. They have a purpose; they are supposed to help the living confront and deal with mortality. They are meant to help us channel our loss and sorrow. They are conduits for our grief.

Grief. Which is a fast-moving river, a raging, tumultuous, foaming river, which my therapist describes as *love, where the object of love is cut off.* Humans grieve all sorts of losses in a lifetime: parents, siblings, children, friends, lovers. We cannot live without love, so we must live with grief.

Death is ubiquitous, mundane, utterly unspecial. Everyone and everything dies. Death arrives as a package deal with life. And yet, like birth, death is special. Love makes it special. When you love someone, you celebrate their birth and you mourn their death.

The death of a loved one is devastating. Its pain is so great, it can debilitate us physically, emotionally, mentally. It makes our stomachs churn. Our grief can make us unstable; it makes us engage in fantastical thinking, trying to will time itself to turn back, to return to when we were holding our love, so that we can smile instead of frown, forgive easily rather than sulk petulantly. But time does not turn back. The dead do not return.

Burial rituals are supposed to acknowledge and hold our pain. They are supposed to comfort us at a time when comfort seems impossible. They are supposed to help us feel less alone, care for our tender hearts as we drown in the endless depths of our grief, frantically trying to surface for air. If grief is water, then burial rituals are meant to be air. We need them to breathe before we submerge back into the water, over and over again. So that we don't drown. So that we are saved.

Muslims around the world have various, culturally specific religious rituals to comfort the grieving. In South Asia, some mourn for forty days. People bring food to the house of the grieving. They recite the Qur'an together, taking turns, so that they recite the entire Qur'an for the deceased in what is called a 'khatm', a completion. Men and women are often, though not always, segregated. Women sit huddled on the floor, or on a hard wooden bed known as a 'takht-posh', covered in chadors and dupattas, reciting the Qur'an, their voices cracking as they both recite and cry at once, breaking their recitation to weep. They hug each other, dab their tears with their chadors, and then return to the Qur'an recitation.

Usually, there are stacks of siparas – the Qur'an printed in thirty sections – piled in the middle of the room. These little booklets of the Qur'an are gorgeous, covered in floral or geometric patterns, brimming with bright and festive colours, gold and silver and red and green. Friends, family, neighbours move through the house of the grieving. Visitors pick up a sipara and read a bit, then rotate off, passing it on to another person who continues reading where the last person left off, and in this way the entire Qur'an is recited in community. This recitation of the Qur'an is like a benediction; it is for the deceased, it is dedicated to them, it is even recited on their behalf. This recitation is a kind of loophole that cheats death; once we die, we can no longer accrue good or bad deeds because, well, we're dead. But when the Qur'an is recited like this, on behalf of the deceased, the dead are rewarded for that recitation as if they had recited the Qur'an themselves. Like this, the deceased is kept alive, for a little longer. The dead are brought back as the sound of Qur'an recitation in community, they live through this recitation.

Often, there are two piles of almonds in the middle of the room. Visitors chant prayers over an almond in the first pile, and then place the blessed almond into the second, reciting prayers hundreds or thousands of times. The recitations, the prayers, the sounds, the tears, the little Qur'ans, and the almonds, all become vehicles for carrying and expressing grief.

In most of the world, mourners do not know the meaning of the Arabic words they are uttering in their prayers and recitations, and this is a good thing. This makes the prayers and recitations effective conduits for grief. Without content, they become canvases, absorbing the colour of each person's grief. The foreign words allow us to give voice to our grief without shaping it, or defining it, or predetermining how we should think about or relate to our grief. We do not have to choose our words, and this frees us to think, to remember, to process, to mourn. The words anchor us as we swim in the incoherence of grief. The words offer us a way to voice our grief with our mouths, to make sounds that express our grief without having to say anything. The words are love, and through them we voice love – love for the one we have just now lost, love for all the ones we've lost, love for the living, love for ourselves.

And we cook, and feed our bodies, which is an act of love that feels like betrayal. But is, in fact, the earth nourishing herself.

Happiness and sadness, celebration and mourning heighten our sense of loneliness and so are best done in community. We need communities to rejoice and mourn with us, we need communities to heal. Even though it can feel that our joy and our grief are ours alone to carry, still somehow, miraculously, community can help lighten our loneliness, help carry our grief. But communities also police our joy and our grief, so while they can help us, they have tremendous power to hurt us. A community's power is at its most terrifying when it surrenders its sensibilities to the puritans among us. The puritans among us are external manifestations of the puritans within each of us.

Puritanism wears many masks, it has many disguises, and its best disguise is us. It resides within each of us and so can be invisible. It is rooted in our self-hate, but expresses itself as righteousness and virtue. Puritanism is tricky because it hates us and it *is* us. It tries to make a moral argument against us, asking us to transcend ourselves. It hates our bodies, our desires, our passions, it hates our indulgence in pleasure, it hates our excretions, it wants to reduce us to the most sterile version of ourselves. It seeks to suppress what is complicated, messy, dirty, leaky about us. But are we even human if we are not these things?

Puritanism tends toward totalitarianism. It demands control of the state, the market, the mosque, the city square. It seeps into our views of religion, nationality, economics, gender, race and class. All expressions of puritanism are inhuman. Because puritanism hates what is human about us. It demands we transcend our own humanity.

One of the ugliest things about a puritan version of religion is that it treats our humanity as an impediment to approaching God. It fashions a god defined by His utter otherness to us. In the face of this god, our humanity becomes profane, unworthy, it is rejected as sullied and sullying. In denying us our humanity, puritan religion denies us love. And so it denies us grief, which is a kind of love. *Love, where the object of love is cut off.*

Puritan religion claims to transcend our humanity, and yet is imagined, concocted by the human mind. So, actually, it is a trap we create for ourselves. It demands we submit, flatten our vast complexities to a stern, unapproachable, unkind, masculine god. In puritan religion, humans are to God what women are to men: weak, dirty, unapproachable unless cleaned and sanctified, polluted and polluting when we are at our most human, and especially at our most female. Its strictest rules, harshest expressions are saved for when we eat, fuck, bleed and die. Puritanism strips away all the layers of human culture that soften and humanise religion, instead making religion rigid and harsh, turning it into something else, a weapon, with razor-sharp edges, so that human flesh cannot approach it without getting cut, without bleeding, without hurting.

Puritan Islam is no exception to this kind of cutting religiosity. Puritan Islam rears its ugly head most prominently and most devastatingly at the major markers of a human life – birth, marriage, death. Puritan Islam strips away all tenderness and kindness from the rituals around death so that they become sterile, unfulfilling. More than that, they become terrifying, they do violence to our humanity, they hurt us in ways from which it is difficult to recover.

The underlying philosophy of funeral rites in puritan Islam is this: life is ephemeral and its ephemerality makes it at once meaningless and eternally meaningful. On the one hand, the connections we make on Earth, the pleasures we enjoy, the sorrows we feel, are all ephemeral. So, they say, don't get caught up in life, don't let it distract you from your *din*. It's not worth it. Any attachment is weakness, a folly. Any hardship you experience from these attachments is your own fault, and a sign of weakness in your faith. On the other hand, there are angels sitting on our shoulders, writing down all our deeds, good and bad, and we will have to account for each and every single one of them in the Hereafter. We will be shackled by what we do or don't do, the choices we make, maybe even the thoughts we entertain, for an eternity. Our actions have eternal impact.

Imams at pulpits preaching a puritan Islam will say that the Prophet asked us to be in the world like the traveller. They will linger on this analogy. We're just making a pit stop, visiting this life on our way to an eternal life, to our home. Imagine if you were on a trip, they say, you wouldn't want to get too attached to anything or anyone. It's best to travel light. But if we stay with this analogy longer, their explanation doesn't add up. First of all, the Prophet didn't say to be in the world like a traveller, but rather to be in the world like a 'gharib', a stranger or a wanderer. Gharib can also mean impoverished, poor. This word for 'stranger', as a cousin to 'impoverished', cues us into the discomfort, the lack of privileges, the vulnerabilities that go with being a stranger. The Prophet tells us to be in the world like the stranger, the one who doesn't belong, the one who is vulnerable, in need of kindness, to experience the world as others do, as new, and frightening, and exciting; as strange.

The Hadith in question continues, with a Companion of the Prophet, Ibn Umar, commenting on it by saying, *When you find evening, do not wait for the morning and when you wake in the morning, do not wait for the evening. Seize your health before you become sick and your life before you die.*

In other words, *live*, now, here, where you are, when you are. Not tomorrow, and not in the Hereafter. The Prophet tried many times to drive home this message, like when he said, *If the end times come upon you while you have in your hand a sapling, plant it.* Even, *especially*, when you think it is pointless, fruitless, to plant the sapling, when you think there isn't any time, plant it then. Because that is when you most need hope.

When the end is nigh, plant a seed.

Islamic funeral rites complete a cycle of prayer that starts at birth. The shape of this ritual is a circle. To understand how it works, you need to know a little about how congregational prayer works.

First, there is the adhan, the call to prayer that is called out from the minarets of mosques.

Allahu akbar, allahu akbar . . . And then, *hayya 'ala l-salat, hayya 'ala l-falah,* calls the mu'azzin, voice like a foghorn, words floating through the streets, travelling, wandering into the marketplace, the houses, the schools, the government buildings. Sometimes the sound is loud, interrupting your train of thought, and sometimes it glides softly, lazily, as you stir in your sleep or carry on a conversation.

Those who intend to pray, when they hear the adhan, hurry to finish the task at hand so they can prepare for prayer. You might quicken your pace if you're making a delivery, clean your plate if you're eating, read a little faster so you can finish a chapter, intensify your negotiations so you can pause at an appropriate place to pray. The adhan announces, *It's time for prayer, c'mon! Come to prayer, come to success!*

Then, just before the congregational prayer is about to begin, there is an iqama, a shorter, less dramatic call that announces, *Get in lines, we're about to pray, yalla!*

qad qamati l-salat, qad qamati l-salat!

Then the prayer begins.

Allahu akbar! God is great! And the imam takes the congregation through all the cycles of prayer, starting in a standing position, hands folded across the chest, then bowing down halfway, bent at the waist, then prostrated, the forehead pressed to the earth, whispering prayers to the ground, and finally ending by sitting on one's calves, legs folded beneath, the body like an accordion, hands placed on top of thighs, turning the face right and left – *assalamu 'alaikum wa rahmatullah!* – to the angels on our shoulders, one on the right, one on the left, a personal surveillance system, CCTVs for God.

When Muslims are born, three things happen to the baby almost immediately. The adhan is called in the baby's right ear. The iqama is called in the baby's left ear. And the baby's mouth is sweetened with dates, usually by the parent chewing a date and sharing some of its juice with the baby, using their finger, dipping it in their own mouth and then into the baby's mouth. The purpose of the adhan and the iqama is to commence a prayer that is completed only at death, when a congregational prayer will be performed for the baby, the child, the young adult, the elder – however long the baby lives. At that final congregational prayer, there is no adhan, there is no iqama. It's already been called at birth. And more, there is no folding of the body, no bowing, no prostration, no loud Qur'an recitation. Just the community standing in rows. The imam calls out, *allahu akbar!* and then, *assalamu 'alaikum wa rahmatullah!*

And then it's over. The congregational prayer and the life. Now, the body can be buried.

God has many names. Two of Her favourite names are 'Rahman' and 'Rahim'. Linguistically, both are conjugations of the root r-h-m, and carry valences of meaning related to the mercy and compassion of the womb. One of the most beautiful things about Arabic is that almost all words come from a three-letter root. And because they all come from these roots, each word is coloured by, carries the meaning of its root; each word is connected, kin, of all the other words, the children, birthed by each root.

The womb is called a 'rahm' in Arabic, and mercy is 'rahma'. This teaches us that the womb and mercy are relatives; they're from the same family, they share some essential characteristics. The words for kinship, sympathy, relationship, love, respect, sparing someone, showing mercy are all derived from the same root, r-h-m. God's names Rahman and Rahim are both derived from the root r-h-m too, and their meanings as the Merciful, the Compassionate, reflect this relationship. If God Herself is mercy, then it makes sense that Her Prophet too would be mercy, rahma.

وما أرسلناك إلا رحمة للعـلمين

We have not sent you except as a mercy to the worlds.

The funeral ritual is supposed to complete a circle started at birth. The circle of life, the circle of prayer; the emergence from a womb, the rahm, and the return to the womb of the Rahman and the Rahim. The earth births us, through our mothers' wombs, then it envelops us into its own womb. Like a birth in reverse. We enter into a womb rather than emerging from one. That this emergence and return is marked by a single prayer is beautiful and profound; the prayer is ushered in by our arrival and it is completed with our return.

In this prayer, the length of human life is the short span of time – the gap, the pause – between the iqama and the beginning of the prayer. This pause usually goes unnoticed, it is gone before we are even aware of it. Like the human life, it is ephemeral, short, fleeting. The place we might overlook as insignificant is where living happens, where life is lived. The rituals of birth and death call our attention to the pause, to the life: pay attention, be mindful. Live where you are, now. *Seize your health before you become sick and your life before you die.*

Key to the ritual of life, of birth and of death, is the sweetening of the baby's mouth with a date. A date first chewed in the mouth of an adult, softened with saliva, and then shared with the baby. The sweetness of the fruit and the human body, both gifts from the earth, mingled together and offered to a baby emerging from a womb. Life can be bitter and sad, but let's start with its sweet. Sweetness calls to pleasure, to indulgence, to love. It says, *I know you're upset about leaving the womb, but there are pleasures to be had here. Look, taste this – you'd never taste this sweetness in the womb. You must leave the womb, leave your place of comfort, you must wander and encounter the strange, be a stranger, and when you find the sweet, indulge in it, take joy in it, pleasure in it.*

When a person dies, there is urgency to bury their body. We emerge reluctantly from the womb, kicking and screaming. And then, like a kid at the end of summer camp, we sometimes end up loving life so much that we don't want to leave. And so we might depart just as we arrived, kicking and screaming. But the body craves its return to the womb of the earth, and so it deteriorates, returning itself to the earth on its own so that we have to hurry up to keep pace with it, and return it to its resting place.

First, the body is gently, lovingly washed. Then it is wrapped in unsewn white cotton sheets so as to have as little barrier between the body and the earth. A silent prayer, a janaza, is performed in congregation for the deceased. There are no words uttered aloud, because words are inadequate in the face of such tremendous grief. There is no movement because what movement could do justice to this loss? The absence of uttered words and movement create space for a community to stand together in grief as they are,

in their bodies, without any expectations, without demanding them to say this or that, to move this way or that way.
Come as you are. Be as you are. Mercy.

The quiet prayer without movement, the janaza,
completes the ritual of life, which started with the adhan
and iqama at birth, called tenderly in celebration and excitement, and ending now with a silent prayer marking our loss.
Then the body is placed in the earth and the mourners
leave. Slowly, we return to our bodies, to our lives, before
our time is also up, and others come to mourn for us.

Puritan Islam misses the point about the ephemerality of life,
demanding abstinence rather than indulgence. The 'real' life
is the next life, it says, and the body must be returned to the
earth urgently, immediately, as soon as possible. And so God
is transformed from a lover anxiously awaiting the return of
her beloved, to a loan shark demanding the return of his
investment.

The burial of the body in unsewn white sheets can be
beautiful in its simplicity, like lovers rushing to remove the
layers between them when they reunite after a long time away.
But puritan Islam sees the simple shroud, made of two unsewn
sheets as a gesture of humility, arriving before God unadorned,
shedding all earthly pretensions. Instead of asking, *How best do
I prepare to reunite with my love?* puritan Islam asks, *How best do I
avoid coming across as arrogant when I appear before the ultimate judge?*

Puritan Islam insists that Muslims be buried in Muslim-only cemeteries. Some people like to segregate themselves even in death. There can be no markers or beautification of gravesites in their version of the religion. Women are prohibited from participating or even being present when the body is buried. They are emotional, they are loud, they cry too much. They'll distract the men from the serious, manly business of burial. There is almost an obsession with forgetting and denying love, and the pain that comes with love, all viewed as signs of human frailty. Love is a promise of pain; that is the nature of love. The rules in the cemeteries of puritan Islam say, *There is nothing special about your love or your pain. Everyone is born, everyone dies. Get over it.*

Of course, Muslims the world over bury their loved ones beautifully, they honour them by gently bathing their bodies, carefully placing them in kaffans, tenderly lowering them into the earth. They plant trees and flowers at graves, they place elegant headstones. They recite the Qur'an for their loved ones. Comfort each other, hold each other, remember and honour the pain of the grieving by reciting the Qur'an communally on the death anniversary of their loved ones. This recitation, like the one performed at death is also called a 'khatm'. A completion. The circle of love and grief are intertwined and the khatm tries again and again to close the circle. Sits at the place where one ends and the other begins. Sits at the mouth of the river, where the ocean of love spills into the river of grief, and the river of grief flows into the ocean of love.

But puritan Islam scorns all these ways that Muslims love each other. It sees the khatm as a violation of its sterile funeral rites, an aberration, an innovation in the religion, a bid'a, a path away from God, a path toward the fire. It sees its own insipid ritual as simple, clean, in service of its demanding god rather than humans and their frailties.

The great tragedy of Sibghatullah's life is that it was so short. A mere four and a half years. Little baby. This beautiful, brilliant life, snuffed out so suddenly. So unexpectedly. And the great wrong that was done to us was that he was buried according to the rituals of puritan Islam. Which is to say, his funeral honoured neither him nor the pain his sudden departure caused, the grief of a love suddenly without its object, in free fall, in a chasm that feels like eternity. This great, expansive love, an ocean of love, shared by so many, suddenly without direction, heaving, frantic, searching, bereft. *Love without its object.*

There is nothing simple or straightforward about a funeral. There can't be. Humans are not simple. Our love is not simple. Our deaths are not simple. Trying to simplify a life at death is a cruel violence. How sacred is life if it should not be mourned?

If God isn't there to comfort us, what is the point of God?

I am sitting curled on the floor of our Baltimore apartment, reading a book on liberation theology in Islam, drinking hot chocolate, all warm and toasty and dry after a workout and a run in the rain when my cell phone rings, blinking its red light. The number is unfamiliar, so I answer with a tentative,

Hello?

No words on the other side. Just the wild wailing sound of a wounded animal, a creature in anguish. The sound of my sister, it turns out. Though I did not, at first, recognise that sound as her.

As I try to figure out where the call came from – an unknown number, I hope it was an accidental call, a wrong number, a mistake – a part of me, it seems, did recognise the sound, and knew that it brought with it incomprehensible pain. I did not want to be so close to the source of such pain.

And soon after, another call. Another sister. This one from Canada, from a number I recognise. This time I answer, *Hey* . . .

I have to tell you something. Her voice is low, serious, grave.

What? I ask, with trepidation.

Sibghatullah. Sibghatullah just died.

Disbelief.

What?! What do you mean he died? Are you sure? Always, in these cases, you want to be sure.

Yes.

There has to be some mistake.

There is no mistake. He is dead.

The initial grief is like wet cement. Heavy, thick, hard to move through. Rumee and I, married for just six months, pack our bags, place them in the trunk of our car, and begin the drive to Worcester, Massachusetts, where my sister is visiting her in-laws. It's a seven-hour drive. Seven hours of bewildering darkness. The drive is punctured by periodic calls from my sister, my sister with the now dead son.

I want my baby back! she wails, screaming, crying. I am crying with her, my nose stuffed, my face wet.

I know, dear. I know.

Utter helplessness. There is nothing I can do. Once you're dead, you're dead.

We arrive at the house that holds my sister at 7:00A.M. The night has passed into day, but it doesn't brighten anything. There might as well be no light, no sunshine. It's probably a beautiful June morning, but there is no room for beauty in my heart.

We park across the street from the house sitting in this suburban neighbourhood. The house is quiet. No movement. I don't know what I expected, but not this. I would rather the house be a ball of fire to reflect the hell that has just been unleashed on its inhabitants. The pain, the anguish, the loss is so intense, so dramatic, it is shocking to see that there are no reverberations, no signs of this on the house, which stands silent, sleepy, like any other house on the block. Like nothing catastrophic has just happened.

The front door is unlocked, and I walk right in. There are stairs in front of the doorway, leading up, covered in cream-coloured carpet. Somehow, I know she's upstairs. Maybe someone tells me. Maybe I just know. I don't wait for permission. My heart will jump out of my body to my sister if I don't move fast enough to keep up with it. I run up the stairs. There is a door on the left, slightly ajar. The sound of crying, my sister's cries, are coming from that room. I open the door fully and stand in the doorway, looking in. The room is flooded with light. There is a bed in the room, which looks huge compared to my sister, who is sitting in a corner of the bed, leaning against the headboard, looking at me. Sheets are crumpled all around her. For a second, there is a pause in the grief, a brief, ever so quick movement, where we both look at each other and I wonder,

Now that we are both here, is Sibghatullah still dead?

Just the question, the possibility of it, lets in a tiny sliver of hope that is swiftly and mercilessly crushed. Yes. Yes, he is still dead.

I rush to embrace her, we hug and cry. The first thing she says, when she can finally speak, gather enough breath to utter words, is:

I'm going to bury my son.

A look of defiance flashes across her face. I understand. She wants to be at the cemetery when her son is buried. When his body is handed over to the earth. She knows that my parents are enamoured with puritan Islam, and according to puritan Islam, women are strictly forbidden from being present at the burial of the body. Until this moment, none of the women in my family has ever been to a cemetery for a burial, and this is a point of pride for my parents. It is proof of the strength of their faith. My parents, we know, will resist my sister's presence at her own son's burial. This will not be easy. In telling me *I'm going to bury my son*, my sister is instructing me,

Figure it out. Make it happen.

I look at her. *Okay. Of course. Of course, you'll bury your son.*

I explain the situation to Rumee. He doesn't understand why my parents might resist. I explain that puritan Islam treats a moment like this – a death, a birth, a wedding – as a test of faith. It's like an exam. If you don't follow its rules now, in a moment such as this, it means you have no faith.

We need to take the lead on the funeral arrangements, I say, *so we can be in control of the logistics.*

Though I say 'we' need to take a lead on the funeral arrangements, essentially I mean *he* has to take the lead on them, because I'm a fucking mess. Rumee, a twenty-four-year-old, steps into the shoes of an adult, calling cemeteries and funeral homes. Trying to figure out how to organise a funeral. Learning what our society does with its dead.

My sister is weeping in her room. Her older son runs in and out, constantly in motion. He's six and a half years old, we're not sure he understands what has happened. My sister has Sibghatullah's clothes in a Ziploc bag, light brown shalwar kameez, with delicate embroidery on the kameez. These were the last clothes he was wearing when she took him to the hospital. She keeps opening the bag to smell them. They still smell like him. She's desperate to see him again. But she can't. The hospital will release his body to the funeral home after conducting an autopsy, and only then can we see him, wash his body and prepare him for burial. We're learning this slowly, step by step.

A few hours later, my parents arrive with my sisters and brother. They drove all night too, from Toronto, through a night of grief, in a green van.

Where's Sibghatullah? Can we go see him?

I walk everyone through the steps. *We can't go see Sibghatullah yet because he's still at the hospital and the hospital will release him to the funeral home.*

Why can't we go pick him up ourselves? my father asks.

They don't release the body to the family, only to the funeral home.

Well, why do they still have him, why haven't they released him yet? What are they doing with him?

They're going to do an autopsy on him first, to find out the cause of death.

No, no, no, no, no! We don't want an autopsy! He's already dead, what difference will it make to know why he died? He'll still be dead! We don't want him cut up like that! Both my parents are near hysterical at the idea of an autopsy.

Rumee explains that he asked the hospital if we could opt out. *They said 'no', that especially in the case of young children who die unexpectedly, they require autopsies. They advised me that it was in our interest to do the autopsy, in order to rule out child abuse, at the very least. So that child services won't be involved.*

We look at each other, confused and anxious. Why would child services be involved? Obviously no one wants child services involved. We can't even think this through.

Once the body is at the funeral home, we will go there and see Sibghatullah. We can wash him there. Then we will take him to the cemetery, pray the janaza there and bury him.

My parents look even more confused. My mother is getting increasingly upset.

Where will the women go when the men are burying him? she asks.

Well, we'll be at the cemetery, so we will pray there and then bury him immediately afterwards.

No, no, no. Women are not allowed at the cemetery! my mother says. She is starting to shake with righteous indignation, her body filling up with air as she prepares to launch into a lecture about why women can't go to the cemetery, why it is especially important to follow the rules at this moment. I cut her off.

Your daughter wants to bury her son. And since it is her son that died, that is what we are going to do.

My father acquiesces. My mother does too. But whereas my father is resigned, hurting too much to make an issue of this, my mother is seething, hurting too, but quiet only because she sees she won't win this one just now.

We stumble our way through the preparations.

Rumee calls cemeteries, desperately trying to find one that will give us a plot on short notice, which turns out to be more difficult than we expected, especially given that this is a holiday weekend. Eventually, he finds a Muslim cemetery with an available plot, where they are willing to let us bury Sibghatullah the next day. It is about an hour's drive away, the next state over, in a small New England town. The volunteer funeral director is away, but agrees to let us conduct the funeral in his absence, understanding the importance of a quick burial. He gives Rumee a list of rules that we must abide by and asks him to sign it. The list is long, and upsetting.

You agree not to raise any headstones or monuments marking the grave.

No one will pray at the gravesite or make any comments other than reciting the Qur'an.

Women are prohibited from being present at the burial.

The list is two pages long, and it is exceedingly strict, even for a Muslim-only cemetery. But the same puritanism that informed the list is permitting us to bury our Sibghatullah right away. Rumee looks through the list, and reluctantly signs.

But, we're not going to follow these rules . . . I worry.

Whatever. He's not going to be there, Rumee tries to reassure me. *We'll just go and do our thing.*

As Rumee is working on the funeral arrangements, the rest of us go to see the body, Sibghatullah's body. When we see him, it is shocking. He doesn't look like Sibghatullah. I mean, he does and he doesn't. Death and the autopsy have changed his shape. His torso has been cut open in a Y, starting at his shoulders, connecting at his chest, then going down to his navel. And it has been sewn back together with thick, coarse thread. It shocks us, how his body has been handled. Crudely, like he was dead. Not gently or tenderly, like he was our precious little baby. Now I understand my parents' resistance to the autopsy. They have seen what it does to a body.

When we see Sibghatullah, we weep. We touch his hair, caress and kiss his face, and hands, and feet. My mother washes his body. We watch and help. She has experience with this. She washes the bodies of the dead women and children in our community, and I am grateful for her service so she can lead us here. This is the first dead body I have seen since my grandfather's, when I was five years old, as he lay on a bed made of rope above a chunk of ice the size of a coffin, in the sehan of a house in Gujranwala.

Once we've washed Sibghatullah, we shroud him in two unsewn white sheets. I'm not sure where we got those sheets from. Did my mother bring them with her from Canada? Our tradition would have him buried like this, simply and without a coffin, but we're having trouble bearing it. How can we leave his body unprotected like this? Turns out it is against state law to bury someone without a coffin anyways, so the funeral home offers us one made of cardboard, for a 'simple' burial. We see the box and balk. We cannot bury him like this, not in a cardboard box.

Since it is too late to buy a proper coffin, and we are feeling the pressure for a quick burial, my two brothers, Rumee and my father go to Lowe's and purchase the necessary materials to build a coffin out of pinewood. My older brother leads them, using the woodworking skills he developed years ago, while building a suite in the basement of our Mississauga home, the first home Sibghatullah arrived in when he was born. They borrow equipment from the store, buy the wood there. They build a box, a home, a final resting place for Sibghatullah's body, in the Lowe's parking lot. They measure and cut the wood, nail together a coffin with love, tears and prayers. Building the coffin gives them something to do. A way to express their love, their grief, their pain for a child, a lovely, beautiful and beloved child. Building the coffin is prayer.

They return to the funeral home, where we are in the company of Sibghatullah's body, and we are relieved to see the coffin, that simple box, not quite a Western coffin, not lined with cloth, but also not made of cardboard. We place Sibghatullah's body in the box crafted by his family, gently, making sure not to hurt his head, tenderly, so as to protect his body – for *us*, so we can feel we are still doing something for him. Because, although we are utterly helpless in the face of his death, soon there will be nothing left to do for him at all. He will require nothing from us. The emptiness to come will be greater than the emptiness that envelops us now.

The drive to the cemetery is long. It is late afternoon by the time we get there. The cemetery looks small, plain, ugly and inadequate to me. We pray the janaza – completing the ritual started four and a half years ago in a room in Credit Valley Hospital in Mississauga, when my mother called the adhan and iqama in Sibghatullah's ears on a snowy night in December. Now, four and a half years later, on a June evening, we are all gathered unexpectedly at a Muslim cemetery in rural New England, about to bury this same child. Who could have imagined this? The women pray behind the men. There is little ceremony, by design. The prayer is silent and quick. It feels like drowning. The light recedes, nightfall approaches.

A machine has removed soil from the ground, making a rectangular hole in the earth. The men place a lid on the coffin, nailing it shut. It hurts when they nail that box shut, another new and foreign pain, as it sinks in that this box, this coffin, will never be opened again. Now we carry the coffin to the hole. My brothers jump down into the grave to receive the coffin, handling it gingerly, as if Sibghatullah is alive but just resting, and moving the coffin quickly will wake him, as if he might feel the movement. And then they come up, they are helped up, grabbing hands that pull them up and out. The living emerge from the grave, leaving the dead behind. We each throw handfuls of soil into the hole. It hurts. We throw some roses down there, the red mixing with the brown-black earth, against the pine-coloured coffin beneath. Sibghatullah's brother uses a shovel to throw in the soil, which makes a hollow thudding sound as it hits the coffin.

We are all crying, weeping, hugging each other. I turn to embrace my mother and she whispers in my ear, in between sobs, through the tears and the pain, *You broke God's law today by bringing us to the cemetery. You will have to answer for this.*

I pull away, recoiling from her words. How can she hurt me now, at this time, like this, when we are both in so much pain? This is the tyranny of puritan Islam. It centres itself so all of our pain is secondary to its demands. Nothing, absolutely nothing, supersedes it. It is merciless. Without rahma, bay raham.

The drive back to the Worcester house where we are staying is long and silent. When we get to the house, my sister collapses on the front steps, refusing to cross the threshold to sleep in the comfort of a bed, under a roof, while her son lies unprotected, exposed to the elements, cold, alone, vulnerable. My brothers carry her in. We are exhausted and worn out. The funeral, as imperfect as it was, is over. We will spend the next decade trying to forgive ourselves for it. A decade healing from this funeral of puritan Islam. A funeral that did not care for our grief. Did not hold and comfort us. A funeral that gave us no path toward healing. More than a decade after the funeral, on my way to visit Sibghatullah's grave, I will voice my regrets about the funeral to a friend, wishing we'd done better. My dear friend, who is driving us, will say, *Weren't you, like, twenty-four years old when you organised the funeral? How could you have done better?*

And I will realise, *Oh! That's true!* We were kids ourselves, we did the best we could. Even if it wasn't good enough, not then, not now, not for Sibghatullah, not for us, it was still our best. And that's worth something. We cannot be held responsible for the impoverishment of puritan Islam, which restricted our imaginations and our choices.

If we'd been raised with another, richer, more colourful Islam, the entire experience could have been different. Our pain and grief and sorrow would all still be there, but looking back at the funeral, we might have more healing memories, memories of tender expressions of love, both in words and in gestures. The funeral might have started a process of healing, rather than another violence that cut us so deeply it took me a decade to even contemplate it again. To look at it and see it for what it was, and not just push memories of it away. The funeral could have been a ceremony for the living, a way to honour Sibghatullah, to remember him. The service, instead of mirroring our grief, reflecting back its darkness shrouded in white, could have offered colour, hope, a path forward. A path awaiting us in the days and years to come, when we were ready to move, take a step, pack up our grief and carry it along.

I don't remember much about the immediate days, weeks, months after Sibghoo's death. I cried a lot. I slept a lot. I was filled with anxiety. I had trouble sleeping. The first experience of relief I had from the crushing sorrow that threatened to obliterate me was a few weeks later – or was it months? I had a dream. In the dream, I had just taken Sibghatullah to a public bathroom, and now we were emerging from the bathroom stall. The bathroom was covered in black marble, polished and shining. The stalls and the counters were black, too. The sinks that dotted the long marble countertop were stainless steel. There was recessed lighting, bright, shiny bulbs beaming down on us. We were at some fancy place. I touched him. He was wearing grey shalwar kameez, with a little white, crocheted kufi. His curly brown-blond hair ringed his kufi, making him look so cute as to be delicious. His clothes were soft under my fingers. His skin was smooth and plump. I took his pudgy little hands and washed them. It felt so good. To see him alive. To touch him. To do something for him. To love him. It was a relief. When I woke, it took me a few minutes to remember that he was dead. But the memory of that dream, how it made me feel, stayed with me. It comforted me, even in my waking hours. He came back, to offer me comfort, to offer me respite from my grief. To let me love him.

When Cain kills Abel, he doesn't know what to do with his dead brother's body. He's sitting with it, trying to figure out what to do next, when he sees a crow nearby standing next to the dead body of another crow. The living crow digs a hole in the earth, then places the dead crow in the hole and covers up the body. In this way, the crow teaches Cain, the murderer, how to bury his brother.

One snowy afternoon, when we were living in rural New York, Rumee and I heard a loud thud, something hitting the side of our house. It jolted us out of our seats, at the desk and the couch, where we were working. What was that sound? In the living room, there were large windows that ran the length of one wall. Outside these windows, lying on the ground, we saw a dead hawk. It had flown straight into the bank of windows and broken its neck. We stared at the dead hawk. What were we supposed to do with it? We couldn't quite bury it; it lay atop at least two feet of snow, and the ground beneath was frozen hard. So we left it there, its body lying peacefully, majestically, on the pristine snow. Then, over the next few days, we watched in horror as squirrels and birds and other creatures feasted upon its body, spreading its carcass, its feathers, bones, red bits of flesh, throughout the yard, turning the snow into a canvas for painting the cycle of life.

We live, we eat, we die, we are eaten. We feed on others; then we feed others. We are birthed by the earth for the earth.

And in this way, we can see our lives as short, meaningless, ephemeral, or eternal, beautiful, meaningful. We are so much bigger than ourselves. We live forever in the earth, being nourished by her and then nourishing her. We are the birds, the squirrels, the trees.

The purpose of the funeral is not just to bury a body. A murderer can do that. The purpose of the funeral is to create meaning, to offer a way to think about death that is not hopeless. Its purpose is to comfort us, bring us closer together, to articulate our fears and sorrows, to make us see how and why our lives are meaningful despite, or even because of, our mortality.

Know this: the funeral is for the living.

It is unsurprising that, given the impoverishment of the funeral ceremony for our darling Sibghoo, it wasn't enough. We tried to make it right again and again, each in our own way, sometimes together, but mostly in isolation. Rumee had signed documentation promising we wouldn't place any markers on the grave, but when we went to bury Sibghoo we saw that, actually, many graves in the cemetery were marked, some with headstones, others with trees, and others still with elaborate stonework. My sister wanted to place a polished granite rectangle around Sibghatullah's grave, marking the place her son was buried. She bought four polished granite blocks and a few weeks after his burial, we returned to his grave. Under the hot July sun, we toiled, digging four feet into his grave, using shovels and pickaxes. When we got to four feet, we were just above his coffin. Just above him. My younger brother kind of collapsed there, sitting in the grave, looking up at us with sad, empty eyes.

He's right here, he said, pointing down.

We mixed and poured cement over long pieces of rebar to create a foundation for the four polished granite blocks that would frame the grave. Then we replaced the earth. We were hurting so much. Our eyes and faces filled with sadness.

My sister was completing a graduate degree when her son passed, and her advisor organised a memorial for Sibghoo on her campus. They printed out a huge photo of Sibghoo and placed it on a stand; people read poems, said nice things. The grounds crew planted two dogwood trees for him because Sibghoo loved dogwoods. This was a few months after the burial, in the fall, so the whole family couldn't be there. We didn't even tell my parents, for fear they would disapprove.

A few years later, my sister moved away from New England. Before leaving, she planted a dogwood tree at Sibghoo's grave, inside the granite boundary. She watered and tended it for months, then placed a laminated sign around the tender, young sapling that read:

Please water me.

When Rumee and I visited Sibghoo's grave shortly after her move, we were horrified to see that someone had chopped down the tree. The little stub of the trunk was still there, decapitated. The sign still hung around the stump:

Please water me.

Motherfuckers! I was so angry and hurt. Disgusted at the kind of inhumanity it takes to chop down a tree with a sign that politely asks for water.

Who cut down that tree? I don't know. It could have been the puritan Muslims running the cemetery, or it could have been someone from town. The mostly white town, where everyone looks at us suspiciously when we drive through to the cemetery and stop off at the Big Y to buy flowers. Racist white people are puritans, too. Puritanism transgresses religious and racial boundaries. It can be a shared value.

The cost of puritanism is mercy. I couldn't bring myself to tell my sister that the tree she so lovingly planted for a son buried too soon was cut down by some heartless piece of shit.

The god of rage is the god of sorrow with both eyes torn out.
—the poet Ross Gay, misremembering
a poem by the poet Patrick Rosal

Sibghatullah's death unleashed a fury in me. My rage was a sharp blade; it focused my vision and showed me the essence of things, allowed me to cut off the fat and leave the meat behind. I burned with righteous outrage at patriarchy, at racism, at social inequality, at capitalism, at how we keep on destroying the earth, even though we know better. In this way, my rage did important work. Often, especially when I was in the throes of grief, my rage felt like mercy. But it didn't stop there.

I burned hot and feverish with rage. I trembled and pulsed with it. It hummed and buzzed in me. I was angry at the useless hospital where Sibghoo died, at the doctors who didn't save him, at the funeral home director who acted like death was normal, at the cemeteries that closed over the long weekend, at the rules of the cemetery that was open, at the ugliness of the earth, at the heartlessness of mortality, at the horror of death, at the pain that brought us to our knees, at how pathetic our pain made us look, at seeing how helpless and vulnerable we were, at the fact that he'd died at all. I was angry at a God who'd clearly fucked up, at a religion that was full of promise but now felt like an empty husk. I was angry at my mother, at my father. I was angry at my sisters, at my brother-in-law, at my brothers, at Rumee, at the third-floor apartment where you had to carry every freaking item up three flights of stairs when you moved in, at the boxes and boxes of books, at my cell phone, at how big the earth was, at how long it took to get from one place to another, at laughter, at the two white women at a park who called the police on my father and Sibghoo's six-year-old brother for looking 'suspicious', at the police who showed up to check if indeed they were 'suspicious', at Worcester, a place with a name that wasted letters by not pronouncing them. I was angry at myself.

The rage was a hardening. It was meant to shield me from the softness in me that sorrow had exposed, a softness that alarmed me. The sorrow made me feel helpless, while the rage gave me a sense of control; the sorrow demanded submission while the rage promised to carry my pain. The rage was just a facade, though, a way to hide the sorrow. And there was so much sorrow.

Sorrow for little Sibghoo. Sorrow for my sister. Sorrow for her loss, sorrow for her sorrows. Sorrow for the colonialism and Partition that displaced my grandparents, rendering impossible countless futures. Sorrow for the sorrows my parents inherited from them and passed on to us, for all that they lost – their lives, their friends, their families, their connection to the land, their faith in humanity for the horrors they witnessed. Sorrow for my parents who spent less than twenty years in Pakistan and then were somehow 'from' Pakistan for the rest of their lives. Sorrow for us, their children, watching our parents spend their lives trying to belong to a place they were barely from. Sorrow for watching our parents unsuccessfully but persistently, god bless them, try to make us belong to that dream place they imagined they were from. Sorrow for watching our parents see the dream place for the real place it was each time they moved back with us, the crushing disappointment, the sting of betrayal, the shamefaced embarrassment. Sorrow for hearing my parents' tense voices as they tried to figure out how to make ends meet when my father was fired by the foreman at his job for praying Jumu'a, for the worry in their eyes as they balanced their principles against the need for a paycheck. Sorrow for seeing my parents pump each other up to ask his brother for a loan of five thousand dollars and the desert their eyes became when he refused – maybe because he didn't have the money himself, maybe because he didn't want to lend it. Sorrow for witnessing, over the years, white people in uniforms – cops, TSA, customs and border agents, doctors, store managers – talk down to, deride, yell, bark at my parents, our gods humiliated and disrespected so. And my parents, trying to maintain their dignity, covering up their shame with rage. Sorrow for seeing our parents through the eyes of white people, seeing their class, their foreignness, their lack of education, their suddenly accented English in the face of whiteness, how the rules of this new country confused them so they looked more like lost children than adults who knew the way. Sorrow for my parents' losing their family members in Pakistan, one by one – parents, a brother, a sister, a niece, a nephew – learning the news written on thin blue airmail envelopes in difficult-to-read scrawl, or on a frantic call with a poor connection in the middle of the night, absorbing the sorrow of lonely mourning in a foreign land, setting their jaws and eating their daal chawal, setting their shoulders and cleaning the dishes, because what else could they do?

Hai, there are so many sorrows. Sorrow for how we were raised, as sacrificial offerings at the altar of an ideology. Sorrow for how little we played and how much we studied. Sorrow for how shame was one of our primary teachers. Sorrow for how the shame is a partition that separates us from each other, disconnects us from ourselves, turning us into islands. Sorrow for how difficult it is to admit the truth of our experiences even to ourselves, and more so, to speak our truths without hurting each other, causing more pain, creating more sorrow. Sorrow for how we repeat the mistakes of our parents. Sorrow for trying to belong to places we are barely from. Sorrow for the multitudes of violences such desperate belonging, such settling, always makes necessary, starting with the pretension that we have the right to be where we are, that we deserve what we have, that we don't owe each other anything, when we are from each other, we have only each other. Sorrow for the weight of failed dreams, dreams of a utopia, of a paradisiacal place which is always a garden full of flowers, now withered and faded and turned to dust. Sorrow for who we were supposed to be, for who we will never be, and for who we turned out to be.

A few years ago, in a rare moment of complete honesty, my mother confided sadly to Rumee, *I ruined my children's bachpan. I sacrificed their childhoods to Tanzeem.*

The puritan in us often expresses herself as the god of rage, but somewhere, deep down inside, she knows that she is actually the god of sorrow. But she cannot see. Her eyes are torn out.

For several years I couldn't bring myself to return to Sibghoo's grave, feeling guilty every time I had the chance but didn't go. Then, in 2015, I got a fellowship at Radcliffe, so I moved to Boston for a year and was able to visit Sibghoo's grave a few times. I made a new friend who was also mourning the death of loved ones. We walked the path of grief together, holding hands, leaning on each other. I was grateful for his company. He helped me see myself and my grief in a new light. He helped me see that the cemetery wasn't as ugly as I had always believed it to be. There was beauty there, like an autumn olive tree, and black raspberry bushes. Together, we lovingly picked out lilies and lilies of the valley from a local nursery in Boston and buried, planted them at Sibghoo's grave. He listened to me talk endlessly about Sibghoo, about his life, his death and his burial. Importantly, he helped me think about where Sibghoo is now. As we knelt at Sibghoo's grave, burying, planting the bulbs of colourful flowers to come, he asked me, *Where do you think Sibghoo is now?*

You mean, where is he, according to Islam? I replied with a question.

No. Where do you think he is now?

I don't know . . .

I was surprised to learn that I couldn't answer his question. Until he asked, I thought I knew the answer.

We were quiet for a while. Planting. Burying.

And then suddenly, I could see him all around me, in the green cemetery, under the bright blue New England sky. He was in the grass, and the bushes, and the trees. He wasn't alone. He was surrounded by beauty. He was, he *is* beauty.

Later still, I took Rumee back to the cemetery.

Look, look dear! Look at the black raspberries growing right next to Sibghoo's grave. Look at the little green lily shoots pushing up through the rich, delicious soil, promising flowers, promising colour and beauty.

We picked off the black raspberries, cute, tender, tiny and juicy and we popped them in our mouths. They were sweet. *Sweet too where sorrow is.* Sweet too where sorrow is.

إنا لله وإنا إليه راجعون

We are God's, and to God we return.

Acknowledgements

اقرأ باسم ربك الذى خلق ۝

خلق الإنسن من علق ۝

اقرأ وربك الأكرم ۝

الذى علم بالقلم ۝

علم الإنسن ما لم يعلم ۝

كلا إن الإنسن ليطغى ۝

أن رءاه استغنى ۝

Recite in the name of your Lord who created
Created humans from a clinging clot of blood
Read and your Lord is most generous
The One who taught with the pen
Taught humans what they know not

Certainly, humans transgress
When they imagine themselves independent, self-sufficient.

All books are written in community and this book was especially nurtured, cultivated in community – in several communities. There are so many eyes, ears, hearts and hands that have cared for this book and for me throughout the years, so much enduring love that has guided and supported what this book and I have become.

Although writing can feel cerebral and lonely, it is fundamentally a metabolising of experiences and a reaching out, a reaching toward; a deep awareness, when we are alone, that we desire to commune, speak to others, offer ideas, write beautiful sentences, share ourselves with others. Writing is about listening deeply and speaking to those who are not before us, who might have passed, who are elsewhere, who have yet to arrive. *Writing*, Robin Wall Kimmerer teaches us, *is an act of reciprocity*.

Those who know me know that I love to share, to be in conversation, so almost as soon as I wrote the sentences in the first draft of this book, and every draft thereafter, I was sharing them, reading them aloud, talking about them with my loves, with my friends, with my family. Reading and listening, reading and watching, trying to understand how the words were landing and how I needed to change them to carry the meanings I meant to convey. Thank you, to everyone who listened.

I owe my deepest gratitude to Rumee, whose brilliance illuminates my world and without whom this book would simply not be. Thank you for the walks, the listening, the sharing, the caring, the nurturing, the reading, the editing, the deep thinking and, most of all, for the loving – for loving all the versions and forms of me; for always, always so willingly doing with me, so lovingly, the work of love.

I am deeply and happily indebted to bbbg. Thank you

for your light, your laughter, your dancing, your tenderness, your ears and sunflower eyes and dil on this book; for pointing out smells and sounds, for showing me beauty tucked away or in plain sight on a well-worn path; for eyes that make the old new again.

I am grateful to all who read this book in its entirety, believed in it, encouraged it, provided me with careful feedback chapter-by-chapter, whose eyes made it better. Rumee (*I mean, goddamn!*); Anver (*take out that scene!*); Joyce (*I screamed when I read that*), Ross (*show us how you get from rage to resolution*), Daniel (*too much is a way of saying not enough*), Samira (*this is a love letter*), Lauren (*the things we are dogmatic about are the things we are willing to sacrifice love for*), Lynette (*we come of age at different ages*).

In 2018, I organised a three-day workshop around an earlier version of this book and I am grateful to the participants who shared so generously of their time, their energy, their insights, who showed me the work the book was already doing in their lives – Sadaf, Iman, Shehnaz, Maysa, Waged, Sadaf, Noor, Samira, Homayra.

I am indebted to all those who listened to or read excerpts of the book over the years, who engaged with it thoughtfully, nourished and nurtured me and my writing, feeding my heart, my body, my soul, and my mind. Thank you to Renisa, Riaz, Sayeed and Lialah (pound cakes and making space for us on your apocalypse raft); Tara, Sebastian, Asmani and Gaia (seed bars, spelt loaves, freshly squeezed juice & huggles); Rosily and Dick (feeding us the garden);

Shakeela and Shehnoor (kebabs and clams and bike rides); Bill and Susan (our adventures, our transformations); Nadia (sharing your story to hold space for mine); Amal (making Vancouver home); Noor and Youssef (hiring committee!); Meher Aunty (impromptu meet-ups); Adel and Nihal (asking me to read more); Minelle (interviews and affirmations); Tamir, Nina and Salma (picnics and plums); Daniel and Kent (pizzas, the blanket and your home); Ben, Lisa, Sophia and Theo (flatbreads and walks); Letina and Solomon (the injera); Naveena and Hassan (newborn daal); Janice and Mary (counsel, coffee walks and dumplings); Allyssa (*it's okay to cry at work*); Candis (exploring freedom); Kim (living openly); Malinda (step counts); Talia and Blair (culinary adventures); Jamie and Ashley (witnessing and dreaming); Vivette and Katherine (trusting me); Iman and Waleed (*Cardi B is Lebanese!*); Azza (insisting on religion); Alia (inviting me to your farm); Tania (the blessing of a dastarkhwan); Doug and Barney (Persian stew); Anna (the bread and the bag); Max (for always helping me celebrate); my sagacious and sorely missed therapist Tracy (*now is the only forever because it is always now*); my brilliant therapist Mercedes (*if love is weakness, then let us all fall to our knees*).

I am thankful to The Rainbow Coalition at Radcliffe, which was one of the sites where this book was birthed. Our care and witnessing of each other was essential for this project – thank you, Joyce (for catching me); Ross (gifting the best reading lists); Sarah (that dumpling dinner); Tiana (encouraging me to stay and look at Mars); Laurence (no party is complete without an online poll); Kris (yoga and knowing when to walk out); Alyssa (teaching us to trust ourselves); Reiko (instructing us through silence). At Radcliffe also, thank you, Michael (reminding me about curiosity, and caring about and for this book); Valerie *(you're a writer, no, I mean, a real writer)*; Elliott (catching me too, and for writing Rumee); Peter (encouraging this book).

There are people in Islamic Studies and Religious Studies whose support has been essential in getting me to where I am. I am indebted to you, Leila, Anver, Diana, Farid, Rahuldeep, Niloofar, Steven, Ziba, Mahan, Ebrahim, Erik, Kristian, Yossef, Andrew, Sa'diyya, Amina. Thank you to anyone who has written a letter for me, unbeknownst to me, who has supported me when they have had power; thank you to everyone who has opened the gate.

I have the great fortune of working in a unit, the Social Justice Institute at the University of British Columbia, that is supportive and kind and generous. I am grateful to each of my colleagues for brilliant, thoughtful exchanges, and always for your generosity. I am indebted to my students, for taking a leap of faith with me, for practising freedom together, for teaching me that freedom is only ever practised in community.

I was supported by several fellowships that made this work possible, most especially by giving me the gift of time. My gratitude to the Radcliffe Institute for Advanced Study, the Canada Research Chair Program, the Peter Wall Institute for Advanced Study, and the Pierre Elliott Trudeau Foundation.

I am grateful to the writers and artists whose work has made mine possible. It is impossible to count them all but I was deeply formed in the writing of this book by the voices, the wisdom, the wit of Chimamanda Ngozi Adichie, Leila Ahmed, Riz Ahmed, Rumee Ahmed, Hilton Als, Elizabeth Alexander, Aziz Ansari, James Baldwin, Asma Barlas, Leroy Little Bear, Joyce Bell, Lucille Clifton, Ta-Nehisi Coates, Kimberlé Crenshaw, Barbara T. Christian, Michaela Coel, Angela Davis, Assia Djebar, Toi Derricotte, Ava Duvernay, Anver Emon, Nikky Finney, Ross Gay, Aracelis Girmay, Donald Glover, Saidiya Hartman, Ziba Mir-Hosseini, Daniel Heath Justice, Tayari Jones, Kristiana Kahakauwila, Mindy Kaling, Robin D. G. Kelly, Laurence Ralph, Robin Wall Kimmerer, Sarah Koenig, Jhumpa Lahiri, Kiese Laymon, Audré Lorde, Kris Manjapra, Renisa Mawani, Hasan Minhaj, Wesley Morris, Toni Morrison, Fred Moten, Mira Nair, Zarqa Nawaz, Issa Rae, Claudia Rankine, Patrick Rosal, Arundhati Roy, Amy Tan, Sonia Sanchez, Sa'diyya Shaikh, Gyatri Spivak, Malinda Smith, Zadie Smith, Kim TallBear, Amina Wadud, Jenna Wortham, and Laurie Zoloth.

A book like this would never see the light of day, no matter the loving care it is nurtured with, unless someone is willing to take a chance on it, which is to say, to take a risk. Thank you, Simran Jeet Singh, for supporting my writing after hearing me talk on an academic panel and introducing me to your amazing agent. Thank you to my agent, Tanusri Prasanna, for reading my manuscript in two days and being exuberant in your love for it; for saying *I don't think I could rest until this book is out everywhere.* I am grateful for your generosity and care throughout this process. Thank you, Anver Emon, for letting this book into your heart and for introducing me to your friend, the publisher. Thank you, Novin Doostdar, for understanding this book and betting on it. Thank you to Vanessa Kerr and Anna Carmichael at Abner Stein. Thank you, Cecilia Stein, my publishing editor, for taking this book on and for believing in it. Thank you to the team at Oneworld, thank you, Ben Summers, for the cover design; Paul Nash and the production team; the communication and marketing teams; everyone who has helped bring this book forth, and will help it yet, thank you.

My debt, my gratitude to and for my family is boundless. Thank you, dear parents, for teaching me to dream, and for bringing me along on yours. Thank you, Mommy, for teaching me the art of telling a story for a moral purpose. Thank you, Deddy, for teaching me to listen and really feel. Thank you, my siblings and your life partners, for all the ways you cared and continue to care for me along this journey, all the little and big kindnesses, countless generosities – staying up late, past midnight, tenderly helping me with a ninth-grade project after yet another fainting episode; moving me, driving me, to New York City, in a van full of stuff, and two beautiful children; taking me flying; oh, that beautiful gift of art on a door, which is a door, always will be a door; and my darling, for the hugs that speak more than words ever could, for holding space for the fullness of our truths. Thank you to my beloved nieces and nephews and godchildren, for the lights that you are in the world. May you tread lightly upon the earth. Thank you, my darling Sibghoo, for all the titlys that you are.

I live and write on stolen land, land of which the xʷməθkʷəy̓əm, səl̓ilwətaʔɬ, and Coast Salish Peoples are the rightful custodians. I am an uninvited settler here. Yet, I am treated with kindness and generosity. I am indebted and I am grateful. Thank you.

And readers, it was fun imagining you as I wrote! Thank you!

Writing is an act of reciprocity with the world; it is what I can give back in return for everything that has been given to me. And now there's another added layer of responsibility, writing on a thin sheet of tree and hoping the words are worth it. Such a thought could make a person set down her pen . . . What would it be like, I wondered, to live a life of heightened sensitivity to the lives given for ours? . . . And just in that moment, I can hear John Pigeon say, 'Slow down — it's thirty years of a tree's life you've got in your hands there. Don't you owe it a few minutes to think about what you'll do with it?'

Robin Wall Kimmerer, *Braiding Sweetgrass*

AYESHA S. CHAUDHRY was born in Toronto and earned her PhD from New York University. She is a Professor of Gender and Islamic Studies. She teaches at the University of British Columbia and lives in Vancouver.